OLD CHARGES
OF
BRITISH FREEMASONS

Old Charges

of

British Freemasons

by

William James Hughan

Athens ‡ Manchester

Old Charges of British Freemasons.

Published by: Old Book Publishing Ltd

Book Cover Design: Old Book Publishing Ltd

Title of original: The Old Charges of British Freemasons

Originally Published in 1872

ISBN–10: 1-78107-182-9
ISBN–13: 978-1-78107-182-3

EDITOR'S NOTE

The Constitutions of Masonrie

? 1704

The Might of the Father of heaven with the wisdome of the Blessed Son through the grace of God and the goodness of the wholy ghost that be three persons in one Godhead be with us at our beginning and give us grace so to governe us here in this life that wee may come to his blessing that never shall have ending Amen

Good Bretheren and fellows our purpose is to tell you how and in what manner this worthie science of Masonrie was begun and afterwards how it was found by worthie Kings and Princes and by many others worshipfull men And also to them that be heare & will declare the charge that belongeth to every free mason to keep Sure in good faith and therefore take good heede hereto It is well worthie to be kept well for that the science is Ancient for there be seven Liberall sciences of the which seven it is one and these names of the seven sciences it is the first - Gramon and that teacheth a man to speak truely and write truely And the second is Retorick and teacheth a man to speak faire Plainy and in subtill termes And the third is Dialectick or Logick and that teacheth a man to discerne truth from falshood And the fourth is Arithmatick and that teacheth a man to reckon and to account all manner of numbers And the fifth is called Geometrie and teacheth the mete and measure of ground and of all other things things of the which science is grounded Masonrie And the Sixt science is called Musitick and that teacheth a man the science of song and voll of songe and Organ tongue And the seventh science is called Astronomie and that teacheth a man to know the course of the sun moone and starrs This be the seven Liberall sciences the which seven be all grounded by one that is to say Geometrie for by this may a man prove the essence of workes as founded by Geometrie for Geometrie teacheth mete measure ponderation and weight of all manner of things on earth for there is no man that worketh any science but he worketh by some measure nor any man that selleth or buyeth but by some measure or weight and all this is Geometrie or

The Constitution 1692

Dedicated (by permission) to the Most Hon. The Marquess of Ripon, K.G.

THE

OLD CHARGES

OF

BRITISH FREEMASONS.

BY

WILLIAM JAMES HUGHAN.

WITH VALUABLE APPENDICES.

Illustrated with Fac-similes of portions of "Antiquity MS.," and the "York MSS."
of A.D. 1693 and A.D. 1704.

A PREFACE

BY

THE REV. A. F. A. WOODFORD, M.A.

(Rector of Swillington, Leeds.)

LONDON :
SIMPKIN, MARSHALL, AND CO., STATIONERS' HALL COURT.
TRURO :
WILLIAM LAKE, BOSCAWEN STREET.
PHILADELPHIA (U.S.) :
CHARLES EUGENE MEYER, 722, ARCH STREET.

1872.

To

The most Honourable

George Frederick Samuel, Marquess of Ripon, K.G.,

Earl de Grey and Earl of Ripon,

Viscount Goderich, Baron Grantham,

Lord President of Her Majesty's Most Hon. Privy Council,

&c., &c., &c.;

M.W. Grand Master of the United Grand Lodge

Of Ancient, Free, and Accepted Masons of England;

This first Typographical Collection of the

Old Charges of British Freemasons

is most respectfully dedicated

By his Lordship's

Obedient, humble Servant

and Brother,

William James Hughan.

PREFACE.

I have been requested by my able and zealous Brother WM. JAMES HUGHAN, to write a Preface, for the very interesting Collection of our ancient Masonic Constitutions, which he has so wisely, and as I think, so reasonably determined to submit to the cognizance and consideration of the Craft at large.

Having been for some time past a fellow labourer with him in the wide and fruitful field of Masonic investigation, and being equally anxious with himself to promote a more careful and scientific study of our archæology and our history, I have been truly glad, however imperfectly, to make this humble response to his very friendly request for co-operation, in his present important and praiseworthy undertaking.

For some years past, as other avocations permitted, I have been collecting and transcribing all Manuscripts which relate to the ancient Constitutions, and Legends of Freemasonry; and I cordially sympathize with Bro. Hughan's meritorious efforts, to inaugurate amongst ourselves a more careful and conscientious study of all those ancient and important documents, which tend to throw light on the history of the past, and to bring clearly and convincingly before ourselves, the genuine claims to antiquity, of our venerable and valuable Brotherhood.

With this view, Bro. Hughan has undertaken, at no little labour to himself, the preparation and compilation of the present volume which, while it will neither challenge controversy, nor deprecate criticism, will, I feel sure, nevertheless, commend itself to every intelligent and conscientious student in our world-wide order.

There are existing in England and other Countries, many copies of what we are wont to term, " The Masonic Constitutions." They are also called by some writers " The Constitutions of the Craft," the "History of Freemasonry," and the "Legend of the Guild."

They generally consist of three parts, 1*stly*, The Introductory Prayer, Declaration, or Invocation ; 2*ndly*, The History of the Order, or the Legend of the Guild, which ends generally with the era of Athelstan, or about 926 ; and 3*rdly*, The peculiar statutes and duties, the regulations and observances, which the Craft in general, or Masons in particular are bound carefully to uphold and inviolably to maintain.

In 1738 in his 2*nd* edition of the first printed copy of the " Constitutions of the Freemasons," Anderson thus alludes to this subject : " The Freemasons had always a Book in *Manuscript* call'd the *Book* of Constitutions, (of which they had several very antient copies remaining,) containing not only their *Charges* and *Regulations*, but also the History of Architecture from the Beginning of Time ; in order to shew the antiquity and excellency of the *Craft* or Art," &c.†

In this statement, our then Grand Chaplain was no doubt perfectly correct, though it is not quite certain to which particular Constitution he alluded or considered the most ancient, as his History of our Order is undoubtedly a *compilation* from more than one of the Ancient Masonic Constitutions.

Indeed he seems, curiously enough, to have followed in some remarkable instances, a MS., of which Krause, a German, published a copy about 1810, but of which the *original* has not yet been found.

One hundred and thirty years, we may say, have past away since our able Brother published his Book of Constitutions, and now as then there are still existing amongst the order many ancient copies of these old Constitutions.

The earliest so far known, is in a poetic form and is to be found among the MSS. in the King's Library, British Museum‡. '

It is a poem of 794 lines, and was transcribed by a Monk probably, or some Ecclesiastic, about 1390, apparently even from an earlier copy.

It was edited by Mr. Halliwell in 1840, and being already published, and still easily procurable, there seemed to be no necessity, to reprint it in this collection.||

This very old rythmic form of the Constitutions, the original no doubt, I believe of all our later Constitutions, has evidently been greatly elaborated and embellished by the poetic taste and imagination, perhaps, of the Transcriber, be he who he may.

This poem has been put mainly into its present shape by one who had seen other histories and legends of the Craft

" *By olde tyme wryten* "

and it seems to be in truth, two legends, and not only one—the first legend

---

† In 1686, Robert Plot, LL.D. in his Natural History of Staffordshire, gives a short account of the Freemasons in Staffordshire, though himself a non-mason, and mentions *inter alia,* "the large parchment roll in their possession containing the legend of the guild, and the laws of the Masons."

He states that this legend is taken *ex rotulo membranaceo penes cæmentariorum societatem,* and goes on to speak of St. Amphibalus, St. Alban, Athelstan, Edwin, and the meeting of the Lodges in York, and that thus, this " parchment roll or volume declares has the Masonic Craft been established in England." (*Plot's Natural History of Staffordshire,* 1686. *P.* 316.)

There can be no doubt, that we have in this statement, a clear and precise description of some copy of our Masonic Constitutions, which Dr. Plot had seen and studied, but of which the original so far, has not yet been verified.

‡ Bib. Reg : 17a ff 32.

|| I have been for sometime preparing it for re-publication with a Masonic Preface. Mr. Halliwell was a non-Mason and many points in it, which have deep interest for us, had necessarily none for him. A.F.A.W.

appears to end at line 470, and then, apparently, with line 471 begins a new rythm of abbreviated use, of the Masonic History. "*Alia ordinacio artis gemetriæ*" There is not, indeed, in the MS. any change in the handwriting, but the rythm seems somewhat lengthened, and you have a sort of repletion of the history, though very much condensed. Whether, then, it be *one*, or is to be divided into two con-temporary legends, it is a most interesting and important Document in itself, and undoubtedly, of the date ascribed to it by Mr. Halliwell, viz., about 1390†

Dr. Oliver, as some of us know, held it to be, the actual Constitution agreed to, at the Great Assembly, said to be holden at York, under a charter from K. Athelstan in 926, and Bro. J. G. Findel sees in it a strong proof, from the "𝕬𝕽𝕾 𝖖𝖚𝖆𝖙𝖚𝖔𝖗 𝖈𝖔𝖗𝖔𝖓𝖆𝖙𝖔𝖗𝖚𝖒,"—in what I have termed the *2nd* legend—of its Germanic origin.

I cannot however agree with our learned German Brother, that a religious legend common then to both Countries, can be held to be a proof of special antiquity to one form of national organization, while I am equally afraid, that the silence of the Poem itself as regards York, is fatal to Dr. Oliver's theory.

All I can concede to them is this, that as it does appear, rhythmic forms of Charters and Grants are extant, which date from Anglo-Saxon times, and even from the epoch of Athelstane, and as Athelstane was the Giver of Charters to various Guilds, we may have in this old Poem, some few traces, still of the earliest form, of the actual Anglo-Saxon Guild-charter to the operative Free-Masons ; and that it is very probable more than one Grand Assembly was holden at York.

There is also among the Harleian MSS. (541 f. 207) a portion of a poem, somewhat similar to the latter portion of the MS. *Bib. Reg.* and which also resembles "Egerton MS. 1995." It is however, apparently only a collection of didactic recommendations of good manners, and sound morals in a poetical form, and serves to show, not only that the Masonic Poem is not a singular form, but also how well founded are its claims to great antiquity. The handwriting, Mr. Sims tells me, is of the early part of the 15*th* century.

The next Masonic Constitution—so far discovered—in antiquity, is that edited by Bro. Matthew Cooke in 1861, and to be found among the additional MSS., British Museum. ‡

This copy seems also to be written by an Ecclesiastic ; or rather transcribed by some learned member of the order, from an older MS.

It is written in Prose, and differs greatly from the preceding poetic form in many particulars, but especially in the more elaborate arrangement and detail of the Legend, which is its main and most striking feature.

---

† My learned and lamented friend Mr. Wallbran quite concurred in this date. A.F.A.W.
‡ Additional MSS. No. 23,198.

As an illustration of this, it will be noticed, that whereas in the Masonic Poem, there are 15 " Articles," and 15 "points" of Masonry ; in the earliest Prose Constitution, there are only 9 "articles" and 9 "points." †

There are also in the British Museum five other Constitutions in MS. and in Prose, viz.,

The Lansdowne, the Harleian, (2) and the Sloane, (2)

In addition to these, there are three in the possession of the Grand Lodge of England, two of which I believe originally belonged to York.‡

There are three still at York—One belonging to the " Lodge of Antiquity," (London) one belonging to the " Lodge of Hope," ‖ (Bradford) one at Alnwick and there are also the " Edinburgh-Kilwinning," and the Aitcheson-Haven MSS. (Scotland).

Besides, there is the very interesting copy belonging to Mr. Wyatt Papworth, one to Mr. R. Spencer, (the original he thinks of Cole's various Editions) one in the Bodleian Library, which belonged to Dr. Rawlinson,§ and one which some writers say, was in the possession of a Mr. Wilson, of Broomehead, and dated from Henry VIII, but of which no trace has as yet been discovered.

Of these MSS. the following¶ have not hitherto appeared in print, (at any rate not *in extenso,)* though one or two portions may have been published :

Sloane No. 3848.
Three MSS. in Grand Lodge.
One at York.
Lodge of Antiquity.
Aitcheson-Haven.
Alnwick.
Wilson's.
Lodge of Hope.
Wyatt Papworth's.

By the kind consent of the " Lodge of Antiquity " (London,) the " Lodge of

---

† I have in my possession, a neat interesting copy of this MS. made in 1728, by Wm. Reid, Grand Secretary, for Wm. Cowper, Clerk to the Parliament.

‡ There are besides the three MSS., two MS. Copies of the Roll, endorsed "No. 1." of 1600 ; made about 1830 for H.R.H. the Duke of Sussex, Grand Master.

‖ The MS. has been in the possession of the Lodge only about ten years. It came to them, it seems, from a deceased Brother ; and of its early history nothing is known.

§ This MS. is *not* in Dr. Rawlinson's handwriting, neither is the original in the Bodleian Library.

¶ A question may fairly arise, whether Bro. Spencer's copy of the Constitutions of 1726, was not transcribed for Cole's Edition of 1729, or even copied from it.   I am inclined to think Bro. Spencer's is a copy of an older MS.   A. F. A. W.

Hope" (Bradford,) and Mr. Wyatt Papworth, these interesting MSS. have been inserted in the present volume.

Several copies of the Constitutions, taken from various sources have been for some time well known, and have from time to time already appeared in print. Roberts led the way in 1722, with a copy which he says was "taken from a MS. written about 500 years ago" and which is in truth, the Harleian No. 1942,† the latest copy in the British Museum, and certainly not older than 1660.

It has also been said both in a French publication of the year 1807 ‡ by Bolieu, a medical man, who wrote the "Memoire sur la Maconnerie" contained in that work, as well as by later German Writers, that there also were some other early publications of these Constitutions.

For instance, it has been alleged that in 1676, there was published in London by Stephen Dilly, a work entitled "A Short Analysis of the Unchanged Rites and Ceremonies of the Freemasons," that in 1712, in London, there were also published "Observations and Inquiries relating to the Brotherhood of the Freemasons by Simon Townshend," and also that the Constitutions of the Fraternity of Free and Accepted Masons of 1689, 1690, and 1701 were printed in one volume, together with the Constitutions of 1723 and 1725. But if these works were ever really published, all traces of them seem now to be lost. No one professes to have seen them, though their titles are quoted by several writers; and up to the present time, no one has produced a copy of them, neither are they mentioned authoritatively by any English writer, that I am aware of.

I have myself spent many a weary hour, in the search after them in vain, and though I will not take upon myself to say, that they never existed at all, yet until some reliable evidence can be produced of their actual publication, we must be content to accept Roberts' Edition of 1722 as the first printed issue of the Constitutions; which, as we shall see later, is only a printed copy of Harleian 1942.

Anderson followed under our Past Grand Master Payne, in 1723, with a Constitution which he seems to have compiled from several MSS. and he put forth a *2nd* Edition in 1738.

In 1729, Cole published an Edition, with a few variations, very much resembling the MS., which Brother Spencer has, with engraved Plates, and issued a *2nd* Edition of the same in 1731. In 1751 he published a printed copy of the 1729 Edition, and again in 1771,—in all *four* Editions.

In 1730, an Edition of the Constitution was published at Dublin, by J. Watts, and J. Pennell, which is however only a verbatim copy of the English Grand Lodge Edition of 1723. There is also a copy of date 1739 printed for Mrs. Dodd

† Transcribed verbatim et literatim for this work.
‡ Annales Maçonniques, Paris, Caillot A.D. 1807.

at the "Peacock" without Temple Bar, London, but it is evidently, I think, a copy of Cole's, and is of no real value or importance.

Last year, Bro. Spencer published under the able Editorship of our Bro. the Rev. J. E. Cox, D.D. (P.G. Chaplain,) an interesting volume of the Constitutions, including the 1722 Edition, the 1723, the 1730, and the 1726 from a MS. in his possession, which is, as I said before however, not an original MS. but a copy of some other in all probability.

Wm. Preston, as we know printed in his various Editions considerable portions of the Antiquity MS., which, though transcribed (as now published in extenso,) in 1686, represents undoubtedly a much earlier date.

In 1794, a copy was inserted in the "Freemasons' Magazine," which was, I believe, taken from Cole's MS.; and early in the present century, (1815,) Dowland published in the "Gentleman's Magazine," that most ancient form of the Constitution, of which, unfortunately so far, the *original* has not been found, though Dowland said he had seen it, and copied his from it, and that it belonged to the 17*th* century.

There was a form of the Constitutions published in the "London Encyclopædia" soon after this which was clearly a copy of Dowland's, and Bro. Hughan tells me, that Hargrove in his History of York, 1818, mentions a MS. as then existing at York, which has not so far, he thinks, been identified.

As I said before, Roberts' Edition of 1722, is a reprint practically of the Harleian 1942; and in 1855 & 1858 transcripts faithfully done, were printed in the Freemasons' Magazine of the Rawlinson and Lansdowne MSS. respectively.

Of later years several of the Constitutions have been printed—especially by my zealous Bro. W. J. Hughan, who deserves the thanks of the Craft, for his faithful and laborious efforts, to advance the interests of true Masonic Information and archæology.

Bro. Hughan in 1869 reprinted at great expense, a lithograph fac-simile of Cole's Edition of 1729, and has since from time to time printed in his various interesting and valuable works.

> York MS. A.D. 1693.
> Harleian MS. No. 2054.
> York MS. A.D. 1704.
> Sloane MS. A.D. 1659.
> Edinburgh-Killwinning MS.†

In Laurie's new Edition of the History of the Grand Lodge of Scotland, there is a Constitution printed, of which, I believe the original is not forthcoming, and it is supposed to have been taken mainly from the Aitcheson-Haven (or Musselburgh) MS.

---

† Making in all (inclusive of those in this work) some fifteen MSS.

There are however in Scotland, two interesting MSS. called respectively, the Schaw and the Eglinton MSS. which are not however Constitutions properly called, but rather Regulations for the workmen and the work.

We have now got to the end of all the known forms so far, of the Constitutions, alike in MS. and in print, but of course, these are not all, independent and original forms, but mainly transcripts or fac-similes of others. Preston's for instance is taken from the Antiquity, Robert's from the Harleian 1942. Cole's *four*, and Spencer's of 1726, all form one family. The Dublin Edition of 1730 is a copy of the English Edition of 1723, and the Freemasons' Magazine of 1794 a copy of Cole's. Mr. Wyatt Papworth's MS. is a copy of Dowland's modernized, and the Edinburgh-Kilwinning MS. seems to be taken from the English Grand Lodge MS. of 1632. Of all printed forms, Dowland's is the oldest to my mind, which was originally pointed out to me, by Mr. W. R. Wallbran, in which opinion Mr. Wyatt Papworth concurs, as also Mr. R. Sims, British Museum. It is clearly from its archaisms, older than any other known printed form, and ranks in antiquity, next to Matthew Cooke's.

I propose now to give the Dates of the MSS. themselves as far as I think can safely be laid down ; partly with reference to the actual date of each of the MSS., and partly with reference to the date of their transcription, though I need hardly remind my readers, that the date of the transcription is no clue to the real antiquity of the MS. or any just criterion of its value considered archæologically.

Indeed it might quite fairly and truly be said, that unless we know how far the copyists of the "Constitutions," in the Lansdowne, Harleian and Sloane MSS. for instance, have modernized the text they have copied from, it is very difficult to assign correct dates to these documents. But making every allowance for the fact of the various MSS. having been so to say, tampered with, that is, modernized and altered in form and verbiage, the following are the dates, which I think may be properly assigned to the different MSS., and bearing in mind, all the MSS. transcribed, even those of a late date, have been derived from an earlier and probably common origin—unless there is any marked peculiarity in them, to which I shall call attention, as clearly demonstrating their early date.

I think it best, where the date of the Transcription is undoubted, to adhere to this in the general summary.

Dowland's Transcript represents a MS. *circa* 1500.
The Lansdowne MS. . . . . . *do.* 1560.
The "York MS. No. 1." (Grand Lodge) *do.* 1600.
Harleian MS. 2054 † . . . . . *do.* 1625.

† The " Harleian 2054 " is nearly a verbatim copy of Dowland's form, slightly later, and must have been transcribed either from an early, and almost contemporaneous copy of "Dowland's," or it is really a copy of Dowland's itself, though made about ten years later. There are words in it, which are clearly older than the date of R. Holmes's transcription.

Grand Lodge MS. . . . . . . _circa_ 1632.
Sloane MS. 3848. . . . . . . _certi_ 1646.
Sloane MS. 3323. . . . . . . _do._ 1659.
Harleian MS. 1942. . . . . . . _circa_ 1660.
Aitcheson-Haven MS. (Musselburgh) _certi_ 1666.
Edinburgh-Kilwinning MS. . . . . _circa_ 1670.
York MS. No. 5 . . . . _do._ 1670.
York MS. No. 6 (Grand Lodge) . . _do._ 1680.
Lodge of Antiquity MS. . . . . _certi_ 1686.
York MS. No. 2 . . . . _do._ 1693.
Alnwick MS. . . . . _do._ 1701.
York MS. No. 4 . . . . . . _do._ 1704.
Mr. Wyatt Papworth's MS. . . . _circa_ 1714.
Dr. Rr. Rawlinson's MS. . . . . _do._ 1720.

I have said nothing of other fragments or allusions to the Constitutions which may be found in many other works from 1737, because in truth, they are all either developments of Anderson's, or modified and expanded from Roberts' and Cole's Editions. Neither do I think it needful to allude further to the articles on masonry and the Constitutions published in such works as the London Encyclopædia, Chambers' Encyclopædia and others, because as I have already incidentally pointed out, such are derived from already known forms of the Constitutions.

There is however in the "Biographia Britannica," a statement which it is necessary to consider. It is there stated that Mr. Ashmole had made a collection of MSS. with the view of writing a History of our Order, and the writer remarks that he saw these collections and legends, and alludes also in Dr. Plot's words to the _rotulo membranceo penes cœmentariorum societatem._

Such documents however do not exist among E. Ashmole's MSS. in the "Bodleian Library," Oxford, which have been lately carefully indexed, and the only MS. relating to Masons there found, is an indenture between the Lord Chamberlain, and two freemasons, specifying the work to be done in vaulting the roof of the quires of Windsor chapel. If any such MSS. of Elias Ashmole's still exist, they are in some private family collection of his papers, but not in the "Bodleian, Library," Oxford.

I have said nothing so far, as regards either the agreement or disagreement of the various MSS., for that would indeed require a laborious and careful collation of them, one and all, which time has not permitted. Some of the MSS. mentioned, have never yet been, and are not now, printed, and until we have them all in print before us, it will be impossible to lay down any absolute conclusions on the subject. But the reader will, I think, be necessarily struck with variations in those now presented to his notice, more or less important differences of order and detail, which it is scarcely necessary to dwell upon, and which require much careful study and consideration to estimate often at their proper value.

It is not because one MS. differs from another, that therefore its testimony is independent, or its authority co-equal, for many of the variations and deviations we shall notice have arisen either from the haste or error of the Transcriber, or from some peculiar local custom, some use of the district, the "limitt," the "guild," and the "assembly." Some may think that they can find, so to say, family groups of MSS. as with the two Sloanes † and the Lansdowne—or Dowland's and Mr. Papworth's, and the Grand Lodge of 1632,—or Cole's Edition and Bro. Spencer's MS.; this may be perfectly true, and by a minute analysis, and careful comparison, we may be able to trace back all our later Constitutions, to one or two main sources.

The Constitutions seem in fact, to be clearly derived from the Masonic Poem, though naturally altered in their prose form, and expanded and modified through transmission, and oral tradition, as well as by the lapse of time, and the change of circumstances.

It we would carefully study the Constitutions to day, in all their component parts and arrangements, subject to certain unavoidable differences of expression and order, I believe that we shall find them most fully developed in " Dowland," from which form, I also believe, almost all the remaining Constitutions derive their phraseology and arrangement ; for it is clearly an independent form, *sui generis*, and is probably the original of all the later forms modernized by the various transcribers. I confess, that the earliest form to my mind, of all the MS. Constitutions, (not excepting any but the Masonic Poem) is the York MS. of 1693 ; that is to say, that it represents in its traditions, a very old form indeed, probably even anterior to 1490, and coœval with the Guild of Masons mentioned in the York Fabric Rolls.

I allude to that peculiar passage in it which recognizes female membership, as that fact points to a very early period indeed of Guild history and organization.

But, I think I have said enough to show the great interest and value of these Documents. Let us hope that Bro. Hughan's zealous labours may pave the way for still further discoveries and still abler disquisitions.

I have kept for the last, a few words I wish to say about a disputed point, namely, the alleged York Constitutions of Edwin and which is given at the close of this work. At the beginning of this century Bro. Schneider of Altenburg, received from a Bro. Böttger then in London, an account of an old York Constitution which he had seen. In 1808, a Bro. Van Dyk from Holland brought Bro. Schneider in Altenburg, a later translation of the same, which he had obtained

---

† Both of the "Sloane," represent a MS. soon after the Lansdowne, if they be not copies of the same original.

through a Col. Wm. Erskine, who was then often in York and which was verified by a certain J. Stonehouse, (with his signature and seal) said to be living at York January 1801.

This Constitution, Krause published † on such authority, (consisting in truth of three parts.) The first is said to be the Constitution of Prince Edwin; the 2*nd*, Duties and Regulations drawn up in 1694 by Command of King William III; and the 3*rd*, Regulations from the time of King Edward, to the time of King Henry VIII.

For a long time these Constitutions were accepted as real and true, but doubts arising, the originals were sought for, but have not yet been found. Up to the present, there is no known MS. which exactly agrees with the 1st or 2nd forms which Krause published; and the 3rd version was quite unknown I believe in England, until attention was drawn to it in Krause's work. Our learned Brother Findel pronounces the Constitution to be spurious, and in this opinion many concur.

I confess, that I do not feel satisfied, that such is a right conclusion, but think the matter should remain in abeyance at present, as I believe we have by no means yet exhausted the list of old Constitutions, unknown so far, but still existing in this country; and it is just possible that Krause's form may eventually prove to be like Anderson's, a compilation from more than one MS. Of course I do not for one moment, accept the mistaken tradition of Edwin, but I am not quite sure, that there is not a "foundation truth" as the Germans would say, at the bottom of our old Masonic Tradition. Athelstan, had as far as we can make out, no son or brother called Edwin—Edwin the Atheling, (or as he is also called by some Chroniclers *Edmund*) was drowned at sea! But the old Masonic Tradition, points I believe to Edwin, or Edivin, King of Northumbria, whose rendezvous once was at Auldby, near York, and who in 627 aided in the building of a stone church at York after his baptism there, with the Roman workmen.

Tradition sometimes gets confused after the lapse of time, but I believe the Tradition is in itself true, which links Masonry to the Church building at York by the operative Brotherhood under Edwin, in 627, and to a guild charter under Athelstan in 927.

I have, I hope, by a similar statement of facts, succeeded in pointing out the true value and the lasting importance of such a publication as this, both to the Archæologist and to every Freemason. Not only are these "Constitutions" most interesting in themselves, as undoubted records of the past, and most valuable from the use of peculiar words, and curious archaisims, but they serve to throw light in a remarkable manner, on the true history of our order, and to illustrate the progress and preservation of our ancient craft.

† "Die drei ältesten Kunsturkunden" (Dresden 1810; 2 Vols. 2nd Edition 1820.)

Even regarded in this light alone, these old legends and traditions, these bye gone usages and regulations of the operative guilds, thus happily preserved, have and always must have for all thoughtful freemasons, the deepest value and the most lasting interest. For it is, as I have often before ventured to observe, in these very peculiar usages of the handicraft assemblies, the local and general customs of the Masonic sodalities, that while on the one hand, we are still able to find, (and there only) the explanation of our own speculative rites and customs to-day ; so on the other, it is by the gradual development of these old traditions, as time ran on, habits changed, new wants arose, and old landmarks were swept away, that we are permitted to advance the only consistent and satisfactory theory of the wonderful existence and permanancy of Freemasonry among us, and its change from an actual operative and mechanical association to a speculative and accepted Brotherhood.

But with these remarks I must close my far too lengthy preface.

I trust, that this imperfect contribution of mine to Bro. Hughan's interesting work, may subserve the end I had in view, in writing what I have, mainly to interest other able brethren in the study and comparison of authentic documents, as it is thus only, believe me, that we shall ever be able to put before the Craft, a satisfactory and unimpeachable history of our benevolent and time honoured society.

A. F. A. WOODFORD,
P.G.C. of England.

Swillington Rectory, Leeds,
March 21st, 1872.

CONTENTS.

THE OLD CHARGES OF BRITISH FREEMASONS.

APPENDICES.

And

That he shall not purloyn nor steale the goods of
any pson nor willingly suffer harme or shame
or Consent thereto during his said apprentishipp
either to his Mr or dame or any other freemason

But to withstand the same to the utmost of his power
And thereof to informe his said Mr or some other
freemason withall Convenient sped that may bee

These be the Constitucions of the noble and famous
Hystory Called Masonry made and now in practice
by the best Masters and followed for directing
and guideing all that use the said Craft, scripted
po me vicesimo tertio die Octobris Anno Regni regis
et Regina Gulielmy et Marie quinto Annoq
domini 1693

Mark Kipling

The names of the Lodg
William Simpson   Cristopher Thompson
Anthony Horsman   Cristopher Gill
Mr Isaack Brent Log Ward

OLD CHARGES

OF

BRITISH FREEMASONS.

BELIEVING as we do that the present Association of Freemasons is an out-growth of the Building Corporations and Guilds of the Middle Ages, as also the lineal descendant and sole representative of the early secret masonic sodalities, it appears to us that their ancient Laws and Charges are especially worthy of preservation, study, and reproduction. No collection of these having hitherto been published, we have undertaken to introduce several of the most important to the notice of the Fraternity.

We have likewise written a sketch of the existing MS. Constitutions in Great Britain, in the hope that ere long their general character and history may become familiar to the members of the " mystic tie."

These "old charges" are of great interest not only to Freemasons, but to Antiquarians generally, as they demonstrate the continuous and intimate connection subsisting between operative and speculative Masonry for the last five hundred years, and traditionally for a much longer period.

An erroneous impression prevails that the *speculative* element was unknown prior to the institution of the first Grand Lodge, A.D. 1717.

The Records of many pre-eighteenth century Lodges often allude to the initiation of noblemen and others, who were certainly not made masons for operative purposes. The election of Harrie Elphinston, Tutor of Airth, as Master of the Aberdeen Lodge, A.D. 1670; and of the Earl of Cassillus, A.D. 1672, and Lord Eglinton, A.D. 1674, as Deacons of " Mother Lodge, Kilwinning," (Scotland) are alone sufficient to demonstrate the *speculative* character in part of early operative Masonry.

B

From the fourteenth century the MSS. mentioned or published in this work have been accepted by " Masters and Fellowes" as the genuine repertories of their time-honoured traditions and regulations. With trifling exceptions, no other Records descriptive of their customs have been discovered anterior to A.D. 1600.

The legendary history and general Laws were occasionally inserted at the commencement of Lodge minute-books, but usually they were engrossed on long parchment rolls† : these had always to be produced on the admission of Apprentices in whose hearing the contents were read, and who, in order to secure their observance of the ancient landmarks, were required to swear fidelity on the "Holy Scripture."

There are at least Twenty original MS. Constitutions extant in England and Scotland, the majority of which were transcribed during the seventeenth century from much older documents.

These must not be confounded, either with the Masonic Statutes of 1598-9, or the " St. Clair-Charters" of 1600 and 1628, and other valuable Scottish documents, which are not accurately speaking *general* " Manuscript Constitutions." The same remark also applies to sundry Masonic ordinances promulgated in this country from about A.D. 1350, for Ecclesiastical purposes, which are still happily preserved, and to such papers as the Sloane MS., No. 3329, (British Museum) which refer more particularly to the *ceremonies* rather than the History and Rules of the Craft.

With these few prefatory remarks we will proceed with our sketch of the " Constitutions."

———

(A.) " HALLIWELL'S MS.," BRITISH MUSEUM, *1390.
(Bib. Reg. 17a, If. 32.)

This curious Poem, containing the Constitutions of Masonry (small quarto on vellum) written about the latter part of the fourteenth century, was first made known by Mr. James O. Halliwell, F.R.S., in a paper on " The early History of Freemasonry in England" read before the Society of Antiquaries during the session 1838-9‡.

---

* An Asterisk through this work signifies the date is only an approximation.

† Sometimes these Rolls were of paper, but in either case the sheets were united end to end, and written on one side only, across the breadth of the scroll.

‡ London, 1840, 2nd edition, 1844.

It formerly belonged to Charles Theyer, a noted collector of the seventeenth century, and is No. 146 in his Catalogue as described in Bernard's *Manuscriptorum Angliæ.* (p. 200, col. 2)

David Casley in a Catalogue of the Manuscripts of the King's Library A.D. 1734, styles it "A poem of moral duties," although the Latin Title is correctly given. This error probably explains why the character of this valuable document was not understood until recently.

The Editor of the Transcript, Mr. John Richard Wallbran, (of Ripon) the Rev. A. F. A. Woodford, M.A., and others, suppose it to have been written about A.D. 1390, while Mr. Edward A. Bond, (keeper of MSS., and Egerton Librarian, B.M.) and Dr. George Kloss, date it fifty years later. As all these eminent authorities are agreed as to its great antiquity, the question of a few years is of minor importance.

It is the oldest version of the Constitutions of Masonry known, and is the only British copy which refers to the "Holy Martyrs fowre†", who are declared to have been

"As good Masons as on erthe schul go."

Its traditional account of the origin of Masonry is substantially the same as in the MSS. to be found in this volume; and the various articles and charges if clothed in more modern language, would pass for one of the Masonic Rolls of the early part of last century. The versifier was most likely a Priest.

The MS. is in the "Old Royal Library" founded by Henry VII., for the Princes of the blood royal, comprising nearly 12,000 volumes; the munificent gift of His Majesty George II., 1757.

(B.) "COOKE'S MS.," BRITISH MUSEUM, *A.D. 1490.
(Add. MSS., No. 23, 198.)

Written on Vellum, extending over sixty eight pages, and still protected by the original binding, this MS. is generally considered to be a very good specimen of penmanship of the latter part of the fifteenth century. Its height is 4¾ inches, by 3⅜ in width, and was first printed by Bro. Matthew Cooke, in his "History and Articles of Freemasonry," (London, R. Spencer,

† These ancient Christian Martyrs are alluded to in certain German Constitutions, published in Findel's "History of Freemasonry." (*Asher & Co., London*, 2nd edition, 1869, p. 21).

1861.) As nearly as the difference would allow, the original has been faithfully re-produced in this handy volume. It cannot be of an earlier date than the one noted above, partly from the fact that the " Polycronycon†," imprinted at London, by William Caxton, A.D. 1482, is quoted therein, and also from the omission of certain clauses customary in MSS., of greater antiquity.

This important document was purchased for the British Museum by Sir Frederick Madden, (keeper of the MSS.) from Mrs. Caroline Baker, October 14th, 1859, whom some think was a descendant of the Mr. Baker mentioned by Dr. Rawlinson in his Scrap-Book written about A.D., 1730, (" Bodleian Library," Oxford‡.)

The Rev. A. F. A. Woodford has a copy almost verbatim of the MS. purchased from Mr. Thomas Kerslake, of Bristol, which originally belonged to Mr. William Cowper, Clerk to the Parliament, and subsequently to the Historian, Sir J. Palgrave. It bears an endorsement, apparently written by the first owner of the document, to the following effect:—" This is a very ancient Record of Masonry wch was copied for me by William Reid, Secretary to the Grand Lodge, 1728, &c."

———

(C.) "LANSDOWNE MS.," BRITISH MUSEUM, *A.D. 1560..

(No. 98. Art. 48. f. 276b.)

These " Free Masons Orders and Constitutions " are contained in the volume lettered "Burghley Papers," believed to have been part of the collection made by Lord Burghley, (Secretary of State, *temp.* Edward VI., and Lord High Treasurer, *temp.* Elizabeth) who died A.D. 1598.

They are written on the inner side of three sheets and a half of stout paper‖ 11 inches by 15, making in all seven folios. Many of the principal words are in large letters of an ornamental

---

† Many of the masonic traditions are contained in this old book. In *liber secundus* we read (fol. lxii.) "Therefore bookes that they hadde made by grete trauaylle and studye, he closed them in two grete pylers made of marble and of brent tyle. In a pyler of marble for water, and in a pyler of tyle for fyre."

‡ "One of these Rolls I have seen in the possession of Mr. Baker, a carpenter, in Moorfields. "
Dr. Rawlinson.

‖ Each sheet contains two " water-marks " without date. The *fleur-de-lis* being a prominent feature in the design.

character. Mr. Richard Sims, (MS. Department British Museum) states that these " Orders " have never formed a Roll, but there are indications of the sheets having been stitched together at the top, and there is the mark of a square piece of. vellum or paper having been used for additional protection. The MS. has only been printed once, viz. :—in the " Freemasons' Magazine," (February 24th, 1858, p. 348). The anonymous contributor, who designates it " a clear MS. of the latter half of the sixteenth century " transcribed the document most faithfully, for on comparison with our exact copy, we were unable to detect any difference, beyond two or three manifest clerical errors. It was *not* printed in the " Freemasons' Magazine " for A.D. 1794. The one of that date said to have been the " Lansdowne‡ " was Cole's Constitutions of A.D. 1728.

Mr. J. O. Halliwell, Mr. E. A. Bond, and other well known antiquarians date the MS. about A.D. 1600, and until the publication of MS. " B " it was thought to be next in importance in point of antiquity, to the Poem of the fourteenth century. The style of caligraphy, and other considerations seem to warrant so early a date being ascribed to it. The Historical introduction is briefer than usual in Scrolls of that period. In other respects it resembles the ordinary versions, and is a manuscript well worthy of reproduction.

(D.) " YORK MS. No. 1." *A.D. 1600.

There were six MSS. formerly, in the archives of the " Grand Lodge of *all* England," held at York, (now extinct) and were so catalogued in the Inventory of A.D. 1779. Until recently only *three* have been traced, which are in the custody of the " York Lodge," and numbered respectively, 2, 4, and 5. On examining three Rolls in the possession of the Grand Lodge, (London) we discovered *two* were York MSS., one bearing the endorsement " No. 1," and the other is evidently No. 6. The enumeration in the Inventory must not be taken as any evidence of the relative antiquity of the MSS., as though the *oldest* is first on the list, the *second* is the latest of the six.

---

† So called, in honour of the Collector William Petty, created Marquis of Lansdowne in 1784. The printed part was dispersed on his Lordship's death, but the manuscripts consisting of 1245 volumes were purchased in 1807, by a parliamentary grant, for the sum of 4,925*l.* (These include the " Burghley, Kennett, and Cæsar " papers).

No. 1 is endorsed " Found in Pontefract Castle at the Demo-lishing and given to the Lodge by Francis Drake A.D. 1736." It is composed of four sheets of parchment of unequal length, sewn together at the top ; the whole measuring 7 feet in length, and about seven inches in width.   It was formerly a Roll.

A copy was made of this document about 1830 by order of Bro. William Henry White, (Grand Secretary) but being imper-fect, another was written by Bro. Robert Lemon, (Deputy Keeper of State Papers) and presented to H.R.H. the Duke of Sussex, K.G., (Grand Master.)   Both transcripts are still preserved, and are kept tied with the original Rolls, likewise a letter from the latter gentleman to the Grand Master, dated September 9th, 1830, stating " that it might be interesting to collate the transcript, said by Preston to be in the possession of the Lodge of Antiquity, with that from which the above is made."

The collation may now be made, as both the MSS. in question are published for the first time, in this work.

" No. 1 " appears to have been the original of at least three of the other York MSS. Its date is partly determined from internal evidence, and partly from the period when Pontefract Castle surrendered to the Parliamentary Forces, March 25th, 1649. The demolition commenced during the following month. Bro. Francis Drake, F.R.S., the distinguished antiquarian, who presented the Scroll to the Lodge, was a native of Pontefract. His Father and Grandfather were Vicars of the Parish; the latter, before his ordi-nation was a Royalist officer, and his Diary of the Siege is still extant.   There is thus every probability of the family possessing memorials of the Castle, &c. ; and the " MS. No. 1," is not the least interesting of those preserved.

(E.)   "YORK MS. No. 3.," A.D. 1630.

This MS. is missing, and has not been traced with any certainty since it was recorded in the Inventory of 1779.

In †Hargrove's History of York, A.D. 1818, (Vol. 2,) there is

---

† Mr. Hargrove obtained his information respecting York Masonry, from Bro. Blanchard, who was the only remaining member of the old Grand Lodge, and who had acted as Grand Secretary for several years.   All the Books and Papers which formerly belonged to the Grand Lodge were *then* in Bro. Blanchard's possession, and are now (with few exceptions) carefully preserved by the members of the " York Lodge."

a quotation from the "ancient records of the fraternity" said to be in existence at York, which differs from the text of the five known "York MSS." We think it very likely to have been copied from the above Roll, now unfortunately lost. The extract is as follows :

"When the ancient Mysterie of Masonrie had been depressed in England by reason of great warrs, through diverse nations, then *Athelston*, our worthye King did bring the land to rest and peace, and though the ancient records of the Brotherhood were manye of them destroyed or lost, yet did the Craft a great Protector find, in the Royal *Edwin :* who being teached masonrie and taking upon him the Charges of a Maister, was full of practice, and for the love he bare it, caused a charter to be issued, with a commission to hould every yeare an assembly where they would, within the Realme of England, and to correct within themselves Statutes and trespasses done within the Crafts. And he held an Assembly at York and made masons, and gave them their charges, and taught them the manners of masons, and commanded that rule to be holden ever after : and made ordinances that it should be ruled from Kings to Kings, &c., &c."

(F.) "GRAND LODGE MS." *A.D. 1632.

This Roll of parchment (nine feet in length and five inches in breadth) is preserved in the archives of the Grand Lodge of England (Freemasons' Hall, London). The date "anno domini 1132" is evidently a mistake of the copyist, and most likely was intended to be A.D. *1632* as that is about the period when it was written.

On the reverse of the Scroll in more modern writing is the following :—

> "In the beginning was the word
> And the word was with God
> And the word was God
> Whose sacred and universal Law
> I will endeavour to observe
> So help me God."

Strange to say, it has never been noticed by any Masonic author, or in any way heard of before the present time, neither is there anything to show how it became the property of the Grand Lodge. "Dowland's MS," subsequently referred to, is very like it, and so is one of the Scottish versions.

(G.) "SLOANE MS.," BRITISH MUSEUM A.D. 1646†.
(*No. 3848, f. 179 present pagination.*)

One of the most valuable documents relating to Masonry, as it appears to have been the " received text " for at least two transcripts of later dates. The "Sloane MS. No. 3323," and the "Harleian 2054 " so closely resemble it that we are led to style them, indifferent copies of this MS. Although there is a " water-mark " (without date) in the paper, that is not of much consequence in this instance, as it is signed by Edwardú Sankey, A.D. 1646. It is now published for the first time, *verbatim et literatim.*

———

(H.) "HARLEIAN MS.," BRITISH MUSEUM, *A.D. 1650.
(*Vol. 2054, f. 29,—by another calculation f. 33.*)

The MS. is in the collection made towards the end of the seventeenth century by Mr. Robert Harley, (afterwards Earl of Oxford and Mortimer) which consisted of about 10,000 volumes of valuable manuscripts, and more than 16,000 original rolls, charters, &c., the main tendency of which is to illustrate the history, laws, customs, and antiquities of England. There are but two complete MSS. relating to Freemasonry in all this vast Library.

The Vol. No. 2054 is in the hand-writing of Randle Holmes, Herald of Chester, who died A.D. 1659, and another of the same name who died A.D. 1700, The contents mostly refer to charters and Constitutions of Chester Companies and Guilds of the seventeenth century.

The MS. consists of four leaves, containing six and a half pages of close writing in a very cramped hand. The " water-mark " is indistinct and bears no date. There are seven *general*, and eighteen *special* charges, as with the " Sloane MSS." It was printed in our " Masonic Sketches and Reprints," (part 2, p. 42), and for the reasons mentioned under the heading Sloane MS. No. 3848, we have thought it undesirable to republish it.

---

† The " Sloane MS." so named after Sir Hans Sloane, physician, naturalist, and antiquary, who conditionally bequeathed his grand collection of 50,000 volumes of printed books and MSS., and about 70,000 articles of *virtu.* These were secured by Act of Parliament, A.D. 1753, for the use and edification of the public to all posterity at the cost of 20,000*l*—a sum scarcely a fourth of the real and intrinsic value of the whole.

The two following folios in the Volume (viz. :—33 and 34) are of a very valuable character inasmuch as the secrets of Freemasonry are referred to in the "obligation" taken by Initiates, and the sums are recorded which "William Wade give to be a free-mason," and others who were admitted members of the Lodge. The amounts varied from five shillings to a pound, the majority being ten shillings and upwards. The fragment on folio 33 is as follows, and was written about the same time as the MS. Constitutions " :—

"There is severall words & signes of a free mason to be reveiled to yᵘ wᶜʰ as yu will answʳ before God at the Great & terrible day of Judgmt yᵘ keep secret & not to revaile the same in the heares of any person or to any but to the Mrs. & fellows of the said society of free masons so helpe me God, &c."

(I.) "SLOANE MS.," BRITISH MUSEUM. A.D. 1659.
(No. 3323, f. 209.)

Sir Hans Sloane has written on this volume (fo. — 328 leaves) "Loose papers of mine concerning curiosities." The MSS. are by many persons : The Constitutions, f. 209, being signed *Hæc Scripta fuerunt* p me Thomam Martin 1659.

Having been paged several times, the pagination given in the Catalogue is superseded by one more modern and correct.

The MS. consists of six leaves of paper, (5 inches by 4,) is written in a small neat hand, endorsed *Freemasonry*, and has only been published once. (Hughan's "Masonic Sketches and Reprints," Part 2, p. 23.)

(J.) "AITCHESON-HAVEN MS." A.D. 1666.

This MS. derives its name from the Lodge in which it was formerly preserved. The Lodge met for sometime at Musselburgh, for which reason it is also known as the "Musselburgh MS." It is now the property of the Grand Lodge of Scotland (*Freemasons' Hall*, Edinburgh.)

Although many Lodges are rich in early Records, strange to say, we have not been able to discover in Scotland more than two MS. Masonic Constitutions, viz., MSS. J. and L. In order to

c

make certain on this point, we wrote the distinguished Masonic Historian, Bro. D. Murray Lyon, of Ayr, who immediately confirmed the fact, and also informed us that " Ane narration of the founding of the Craft of Masonry, and by whom it hath been cherished " printed in Bro. Laurie's History of Freemasonry (Edinburgh, 1859) is a modern, (and somewhat imperfect) rendering of the MS. J., and therefore not a safe text to be followed.   Bro. Lyon considers both the Scottish MSS.† to be productions of the sister Kingdom.   Considerable importance cannot fail to be attached to these documents from the fact that they were accepted as authentic, by the Brethren in Scotland during the seventeenth Century.   One contains the clause " *liedgeman to the King of England*," and the two differ but little from the English versions.

The " Aitcheson Haven " MS. we should state is engrossed in the minute Book of the Lodge, and is dated 29th May, A.D. 1666.

———

(K.) "YORK MS. No. 5." *A.D. 1670.

These " Constitutions and Regulations " (hitherto unpublished) are written on a long Roll of Paper, (7½ feet by 8 inches) and contain neither date nor signature.¹ The beginning is imperfect at the present time, but from the account of Lamech's family, the narrative is unbroken.

We have been supplied with a certified transcript, through the kindness of Bros. William Cowling, and Ralph Davison, (distinguished members of the " York Lodge," in which the MS. is located,) and after a careful examination, pronounce it to be a copy of No. 1. (MS. D.)

It clearly indicates the nature of " yᵉ booke," on which the Apprentices were sworn to secrecy : the document is valuable on that account, because with only two or three exceptions, the various versions simply state that "It is a great perill for a man to forsweare himselfe on *a* Booke," whereas this MS. and other York MSS. declare *that* Book to be " yᵉ holy Scripture."

The "Harleian MS." No. 1942 although it does not mention *the* Book, speaks of its "holy contents." The other MSS. (omitting A and B) are indefinite, and unless the context be perused, it is impossible to decide to which Book the writers refer.

———

(L.) "EDINBURGH-KILWINNING" MS. *A.D. 1670.

The MS. was printed in "Masonic Sketches and Reprints" (Part 2. p. 50.) from a copy made for us by Bro. D. Murray Lyon ; and is written in a small quarto minute book belonging to the famous Scottish Lodge "Mother Kilwinning."

Bro. Lyon, whilst examining the Records of the ancient "Lodge of Edinburgh" from Dec., 1665 to Mar., 1671, noticed that the writing was the same as the transcript of the "Constitutions" in the Kilwinning Lodge Minute-Books. This is important, as it tends to fix the date (within a few years) of this "Narration of the Founding of the Craft," and the channel through which it came.

The MS. agrees with the text of the "Grand Lodge MS." (F.) In fact it would pass as an indifferent copy of the document, so trifling are the variations from that important version. An exact copy will be inserted in Bro. Lyon's History of the Lodge of Edinburgh, now in course of publication ; in consequence of which we have omitted it from this collection of the "Old Charges."

———

(M.) "HARLEIAN MS." BRITISH MUSEUM.
*A.D. 1670. (*Vol. 1942.*)

This MS. contains the fullest information of any that we are aware of, and is of great value and importance in consequence. The "New Articles" are not dated, and are peculiar to this MS., although they have been reprinted we believe, from this document several times from A.D. 1722. In Roberts' Edition of the Constitutions (*which we consider to be a transcript of the Harl. MS. 1942)* published A.D. 1722 ; the "New Articles" are said to have been agreed on, at a General Assembly, held on the *eighth* day of December, 1663, and in Dr. Anderson's Constitutions of

A.D. 1738[+], and later additions, they are declared to have been established at the " Feast of St. John's Day, 27th Dec., 1663," under the Grand Mastership of the Earl of St. Albans.   No evidence has been found as yet for either of these statements, and the character of Dr. Anderson as an accurate Historian is certainly not improved, by his having unwarrantably introduced a *modern* Title in the 5th clause, viz., " Grand Master ; " which we need hardly state, is not in the original.

Bro. Henry Phillips, in the " Freemasons' Quarterly Review " (A.D. 1836, p. 288) gave what was then considered a correct copy of MS. Vol. 1942, (Harl.) but on comparing it with a certified transcript, we find that the copyist has performed his task in a most indifferent manner, and actually left out the whole of the " Apprentice Charge," which, so far, has only been found in that MS., the *York* MS. A.D. 1693, the *Hope* MS. (N) and the printed copy of Roberts' A.D. 1722.

(N.) " HOPE, MS." *A.D. 1680.

The MS. now made known for the first time, in possession of the " Lodge of Hope," Bradford, is scarcely less valuable than the *Harleian*, (1942), and is, in all probability, slightly older than the *York*, of A.D. 1693, which it so closely resembles.   The parchment Roll on which this " Constitution " is written, is defaced and worn away towards the end of the " Apprentice charge "[‡] ; (which " charge " is only to be found in three known MSS.), and in its present state, is six feet long, and six inches wide.   The Transcript, which we publish, belongs to Bro. Woodford, and has been duly examined and compared with the original

---

[+] 2nd Edition of the Laws of the Grand Lodge of England.   In the 1st edition of A.D. 1723, the " New Articles " are not once alluded to.   Although Roberts' version was issued one year earlier than Dr. Anderson's, the latter work was submitted to the approval of the Grand Lodge in MS., prior to the publication of the former, which probably explains Dr. Anderson's silence on the subject, A.D. 1723.

[‡] The missing clauses supplied from the York MS. of A D. 1693, are as follows :—
" He shall not commit adultery in any man's house where he shall worke or be tabled."
" He shall not purloyn nor steale the goods of any person nor willingly suffer harme or shame, or consent thereto during his said Apprenticeship, either to his Master, or Dame or or any other *freemason*.   But to withstand the same to the utmost of his power, and thereof to informe his said Master or some other *freemason* with all convenient speed that may be."

" These be the Constitutions of the noble and famous History called Masonry made and now in practice by the best Masters and Fellowes for directing and guideing all that use the said craft."

Scroll by the Master of the Lodge, Bro. Wm. W. Barlow, to whom we are indebted for permission to have it printed.

This MS. and the one of A.D. 1693, at York, are so nearly alike, that it is quite unnecessary for us to publish more than the " Hope" version.

———

(O.) "YORK MS., No. 6." *A.D. 1680.

Until recently supposed to be missing, but now believed by us to be in the custody of the Grand Lodge of England, (London), this Roll has been lost sight of, for about a century ; at least we have not discovered any reference to it since A.D. 1779, when it was catalogued as follows, " A Parchment Roll of charges, whereof the bottom part is *awanting*" *(York Inventory.)* We cannot find any number endorsed on the Scroll in Grand Lodge, but as the writing is partly defaced that circumstance of itself would not disprove its York origin.

Its identity appears to us certain, from the fact that the " *bottom part*" has been severed from the Roll, and though at the present time it is kept rolled around the major portion, in all probability it was wanting when the Inventory of A.D. 1779 was made.

That the present conclusion to the charges is the counterpart of the long Roll, is manifest from the fact, that the parchment is cut through a line of the writing relating to the " Conduct of Masters and Fellows," and *is rendered illegible, unless the two parts are in juxtaposition.*

The MS. (O) is a copy of one of the earlier York Rolls, about a third has been re-written in a most imperfect manner by a later scribe, who, no doubt, intended his performance to be a fac-simile of the faded original : the remainder is a good specimen of the seventeenth century caligraphy.

The document itself contains nothing special, but the conclusion, which we believe to be unique, viz.—

"Doe all as you would be done unto, and I beseech you at every meeting and assembly you pray heartily for all christians— Farewell "

(P.) "ANTIQUITY MS." A.D. 1686.

This celebrated MS. written on parchment (never before prin-
ted† *in extenso*) is in the possession of the Lodge of Antiquity,
Freemason's Hall, London, and is in a better state of preservation
than any others we have seen.   Bro. William Preston in " Illustrations of Masonry" (London, A.D., 1788) incorrectly quotes the
portion known as the " Edwine Charges."   The original clauses
do *not* refer to any " Charges and Covenants that ought to be read
at the installment of Master," although the author declares such
to be the case.   We mention this fact because it has been considered, that a peculiar ceremony was observed at the election and
appointment of *Master* Masons, during the seventeenth century
—whereas no evidence exists of such a custom.   Bro. E. Jackson
Barron had an exact transcript made of this MS., and after being
collated by him, kindly forwarded the same for publication in this
work, and likewise the following interesting account of the document itself : two special favours which we highly appreciate, and
beg *most gratefully* to acknowledge.

*A Description of MS. copy of the Constitutions
belonging to the Lodge of Antiquity, No. 2, London,
By E. Jackson Barron, F.S.A., P.M. and Sec. of the Lodge.*

The MS. copy of the Charges of Freemasons is on a roll of
parchment, nine feet long, by eleven inches wide ; the Roll being
formed of four pieces of parchment glued together, and some few
years ago it was partially mounted (but not very skilfully) on a
backing of parchment for its better preservation.

The Rolls are headed by an engraving of the Royal Arms after
the fashion usual in deeds of the period ; the date of the engraving in this case being fixed by the Initials at the top I. 2. R.

Under this engraving are emblazoned in separate shields, the
Arms of the City of London, which are too well known to require
description, and the Arms of the Masons Company of London,—
*Sable on a Chevron between three Castles argent, a pair of compasses
of the first surrounded by appropriate mantling.*

The writing is a good specimen of the ordinary law writing of
the time, interspersed with words in text.   There is a margin of
about an inch on the left side which is marked by a continuous

† The original capitals, orthography and punctution have been exactly reproduced in our
transcript.

double red-ink line throughout, and there are similar double lines down both edges of the parchment. The letter U is used throughout the MS. for V, with but two or three exceptions.

As will be perceived by reference to the note at the end of the MS., it purports to have been written by " Robert Padgett, Clerke to the Worshippfull Society of the Freemasons of the City of London, in the second yeare of the Raigne of our most Gracious Soveraigne Lord King James the second of England, &c., Annoq Domini 1686."

It is not now proposed to enter into the question whether the Roll did or did not originally belong to the Worshipful Company of Masons ; its interest to Freemasons being a matter in many respects distinct from that point, and the writer simply confines himself to stating that there can be no doubt that it is an authentic MS. of the date mentioned.

(Q.) "YORK MS.," No. 4. A.D. 1693.

In one respect the above MS. differs from all others, viz., in the provision made for the admission of females. The clause immediately precedes the ordinary Craft Regulations, and is as follows :—

> "The one of the elders takeing the Booke
> and that *hee* or *shee* that is to be made mason
> shall lay their hands thereon
> and the charge shall bee given "

We believe it likely that women were admitted as members of the old masonic Guilds, (when their husbands, or fathers were deceased,) if they were in a position to carry on their Trade. We are not however in possession of any evidence, confirmatory of their participation in the " *mysterie,*" or secrets of Freemasonry, and *a priori*, we do not think it probable that they ever did, because the esoteric customs of the Fraternity were primarily connected with the Art of Building, the initiation of Apprentices, and the management of the Craftsmen ; duties certainly not of a feminine character, and therefore wisely restricted to males.

These remarks, however, apply only to such Trades as were peculiarly fitted for men, and not to any in which females were as useful as males. Of the latter class, in olden times scarcely five out of the five hundred were not composed equally of both sexes. In the Guild of the Fullers at Lincoln, founded A.D. 1297, the men were permitted to work in company with the "wife of a Master or her handmaid," and like the Guild of the Tailors, instituted of the same city A.D. 1346, the "Bretheren and Sisteren" participated equally in the beneficial position of the Society.†

Bro. D. Murray Lyon informs us that in the case of female membership in Scottish Incorporations, the freedom of the Craft, carried with it no right to a voice in the administration of their affairs: that able writer because of this fact and other reasons, considers the clause under notice, (in the York M.S.) to be an interpolation, and should read " hee or they," instead of ; hee or *shee.* As it is the only known Manuscript which contains such a provision, it will be well to suspend judgment until further researches have been made. At all events the copyist was certainly a good scribe, and not one likely to make an important addition to the usual Rolls, without some authority at least.

Bro. William Cowling, of York, has, in a most efficient manner, traced a portion of this MS., also of the York MS. No. 2, and we have, in consequence, been enabled to present to the Craft fac-simile lithographs of portions of these two very interesting documents.

The foregoing MS. was written by Mark Kypling, and the names of either the officers, or members of the Lodge (probably the managing Committee) are attached to the Roll, which is composed of Paper slightly mutilated, (10½ feet by 6 inches) and was given to the "Grand Lodge, of York, 1777, by Brother George Walker, of Wetherby."

The "Apprentice Charge," considered to be peculiar to this MS. has since been discovered in the "Harleian 1942," and the "Hope" MSS. Evidently the Apprentices were required according to this charge, (which was composed of ten clauses), to serve their Master or *Dame,* as the case may be ; thus there is *prima facie,* evidence of females occupying the position of Employers, and therefore it is probable they were in some respects accounted members of the Masonic Body.‡

---

† On this subject the Masonic Student should consult Toulmin Smith's "English Gilds." (Trubner, London, 1870.)

‡ The "Lodge of Edinburgh" by a special resolution, April 17th, 1683, permitted widows " to have the benefite of the work offered them by ancient customers of the deceased husband," and the "Ayr Squaremen Incorporation enacted" that every freman's doghter shall pay in all tyme comeing to the deacone and this tred *for hir fredome,* the soume of aught pound scotts."

(R.) "ALNWICK MS." A.D. 1701.

" The Masons' Constitutions" written on the twelve pages preceding the Records of the "Company and Fellowship of Freemasons of a Lodge held at Alnwicke," are of the year 1701. The minutes commence Sep. 29th, 1701, "*being the Generall head meeting Day*," at which Assembly several important "Orders to be observed" were agreed on. The records ranging from 1703 to 1757 mostly refer to indentures, fines, and initiations ; the Lodge from first to last remaining true to its operative origin : the members were required annually to "appear at the Parish Church, of Alnwicke with their *approns* on, and common squares as aforesaid, on St. John's Day in Christmas, when a sermon was provided and preached by some clergyman at their appointment." (A.D. 1708.)

This interesting folio volume, belongs to Bro. Edwin Thew Turnbull, of Alnwick, who in the most obliging manner lent it to us for perusal and publication. A sketch of the Laws and Minutes of the Old Lodge may be found in the "Freemason"†; (London, Geo. Kenning,) and an exact transcript which we made of the "Constitutions," is published in the American Edition of "Masonic Sketches and Reprints," (Mas. Pub. Co., New York, 1871.) under the Editorship of Bro. Robert Macoy.

(S.) "YORK MS. No. 2." A.D. 1704.

This Roll, which is the most modern of the York MSS., is written on parchment, measures 60 inches, by 7½, and was presented by Robert Preston to Daniel Moult, A.D. 1704.

The *Anagrame* is similar to No. 1, MS. (D.) Bro. Findel in his History of Freemasonry mentions that he could not decipher it, but he must have glanced at it very casually, or he would easily have done so. In the same excellent work, a few extracts are given from the MS. which, however, are not exactly quoted. The Roll resembles all the York MSS., but No. 4, which is unique in some respects. Transcripts of it, and the one of A.D. 1693 are still in print, and form part of the Appendix to our "History of Freemasonry at York" in the "Masonic Annual," which publication‡ is sold in aid of the *Benevolent Fund* of the "Kingston Lodge," No. 1010, Hull.

---

† January 21st, 1871.
‡ Geo. Kenning, London : M. C. Peck and Son, Hull.

Cole's copy sowewhat resembles the "Edinburgh-Kilwinning" MS. (unless when clauses are introduced alike foreign to all the MSS.) and for that reason we have placed the letter (L) before the Title. We do not, however, believe it to be a faithful transcript of any Masonic Roll.

———

(U.) "DR. ANDERSON'S MS." *Printed* A.D. 1723.

The Historical Introduction to the various Laws promulgated by the Grand Lodge of England from A.D. 1723, and first made known by the Rev. James Anderson, D.D., are simply amplifications of the MS. Constitutions then extant, and it may truly be said that the value of the Historical Introduction by Dr. Anderson and other contributors, has been materially diminished by fanciful additions to these ancient charges.

The Volume of A.D. 1723 is styled "The Charges of a Free-Mason Extracted from The Ancient Records of Lodges beyond sea, and of those in England, Scotland, and Ireland for the use of the Lodges in London. To be read at the making of new Brethren, or when the Master shall order it," and it is likewise stated that "All the valuable Things of the Old Records were retained, the Errors in History and Chronology corrected, the false Facts and the improper words omitted, and the whole digested in a new and better method."

We should have felt more grateful to Dr. Anderson for his labours on behalf of our Society in furnishing us with reproductions of the ancient Constitutions, and with his own views respecting them ; *provided he had kept these entirely distinct*, the one from the other.

At page 31, the author quotes "A certain Record of Free-masons written in the reign of Edward IV., about An. Dom. 1475, seen and perused by our late Sovereign King Henry VI." This extract perpetuates the "Edwin tradition," and states that the Prince held a *General* Lodge at York as Grand Master. In the subsequent editions of the "Book of Constitutions" from 1738 to 1784, the "*General* Lodge" is altered to "*Grand Lodge, A.D. 926*" with just as little authority for the change, as there was for the Title *Grand* Master in the first edition of the work.

Bro. William Preston quotes the Record in his "Illustrations of

Masonry "† and adds that it is " said to have been in the possession of the famous Elias Ashmole, and unfortunately destroyed."
Nothing, however, is said of such a catastrophe having occurred,
in the " 1723 Constitutions."

Another MS. is alluded to, and partly quoted by Dr. Anderson
at page 34, and appears to us simply an extract from " Cooke's
MS.," (B.) as it is almost word for word, and is not to be found
in any other existing MS.

The part transcribed refers to the Sheriff, Mayor, or Alderman
joining the Lodge " to uphold the Master and Wardens against
Rebels, and for upbearing the Rights of the Realm." There are
only two MSS. mentioned in the 1723 Edition, one of which we
believe is Cooke's MS., (or probably the copy formerly in the
possession of William Cowper 1728,) and the other we have
termed *Dr. Anderson's MS.* ; and added the prefix (U) for con-
venience of reference.

A more lengthy quotation from the one we deem " Cooke's
MS.," is printed in the *2nd* Edition of the Constitutions (A.D.
1738, p. 71,) the first part of which is said by Dr. Anderson and
William Preston, to belong to the reign of Edward III., and the
remaining portion is declared by the latter Brother to be " a very
old MS., of which a copy is said to have been in the possession of
the late George Payne, Esq., Grand Master in 1718."

The quotation is not divided in the " Book of Constitutions" ;
and the most probable explanation is, that Bro. George Payne was
at one time the owner of Cooke's MS. ; which was transcribed
for William Cowper aforesaid, and after passing through several
hands, has at length become the property of Bro. Woodford.

A *third* MS. is noticed in this Edition of the Constitutions, ‡
viz. :—

(V.) "STONE'S MS." *Printed* A.D. 1738,

and is thus described " An old MS. which was destroyed with
many others in 1720, said to have been in the possession of
Nicholas Stone, a curious sculptor under Inigo Jones." The
wages recorded, differ from MSS. generally ; the only versions
that we are aware of, which agree with this copy being the " Edinburgh Kilwinning," Krause's and Cole's. The portion printed
is as follows :—

---

† London, A.D. 1788, page 182.
‡ A.D. 1738, p. 57. Preston's " Illustrations," A.D. 1788, p. 174, and other works.

" St. Alban loved *Masons* well, and cherished them much, and he made their pay right good, *viz.: Two Shillings per Week, and Three Pence to their Cheer ;* whereas before that Time, through all the Land, *a Mason had but a Penny a Day, and his Meat*, until *St. Alban amended it.* He also obtained of the King a charter for the *Free Masons*, for to hold a general council, and gave the name of *Assembly*, and was thereat himself as *Grand Master* and helped to make *Masons*, and gave them Good Charges, &c."†

(W.) "DOWLAND'S MS." *Printed*, A.D. 1815,

In the Gentleman's Magazine for A.D. 1815‡ was published a copy of an ancient MS. of great value. We think it likely the original will after careful comparison be traced to one of the MSS. extant. Mr. James Dowland forwarded it to the Editor with the following remarks. " For the gratification of your readers, I send you a curious address respecting Freemasonry which not long since came into my possession. It is written on a long roll of parchment, in a very clear hand apparently in the 17th century, and probably was copied from a MS. of earlier date."

Bro. Woodford, Mr. Wallbran, Mr. Sims, and other eminent authorities consider the *original of the copy* from which the transcript for the " Gentleman's Magazine " was written, to be a scroll of at least a century earlier than the date ascribed to Mr. Dowland's MS. and in consequence date it about A.D. 1550, or in other words, next in point of antiquity to MS. B.

The text differs but little from the " Grand Lodge " and " Edinburgh-Kilwinning " MSS., and the amount of Wages recorded agrees with the former MS., as also with some of the York MSS.

The last copy of the "Constitutions" we have to notice of those printed in Great Britain, the *originals* of which are at present missing, is

(X.) "Dr. RAWLINSON'S MS.," *Printed* A.D. 1855.

The transcript of this Manuscript, formerly the property of Bro. Richard Rawlinson, LL.D., is in a " Scrap Book " preserved in the Bodleian Library, Oxford, the contents of which vary in date from about 1720 to 1740. Bro. the Rev. J. Sidebotham, B.A. copied and published it in the " Freemasons' Monthly Magazine," for A.D. 1855.‖ It has generally been considered that the

---

† Dr. Plot, in his "History of Staffordshire," A.D. 1686, quotes from a "Schrole of Parchment " on masonry, but not *verbatim et literatim*

‡ May 31st, page 489. ‖ March, *page* 151, and April, *page* 209.

original (written about A.D. 1700) was in the Bodleian Library ; but on noticing that the copyist had entered above the transcript, in the *Scrap Book* " Copied from an old MS. in the possession of Dr. Rawlinson," we communicated with Bro. Alderman Spiers, F.S.A., of Oxford, who after due enquiry, informed us that the MS. itself has not been discovered.

We hope, however, by the renewed researches of zealous Brethren, the foregoing document, and other missing Masonic Scrolls will be found, as it is very probable several such MSS. still remain unnoticed in the muniment rooms of Public and Private Libraries in this country. It is only lately that any complete copies [†] of the MS. Masonic Constitutions extant, have been published, and until the last few years, not half the Masonic Rolls now traced, were even known to be in existence.

Of Masonic MSS. formerly known, but of which no portion has ever been printed, or transcribed, there is but one, viz.,

(Y.) "WILSON'S MS." (About A.D. 1520.)

The first reference to it that we can find, is by the author of the " Manifesto of the Lodge of Antiquity," A.D. 1778, wherein he mentions "an old MS. in the hands of Mr. Wilson, of Broomhead, near Sheffield, Yorkshire, written in the reign of King Henry VIII." It is not alluded to in the first Edition of Hutchinson's " Spirit of Masonry," A.D. 1775, as some writers have stated, but in later works it is occasionally noted.

The " Constitutions " selected for publication in this Volume, comprise transcripts of all the original MSS. of note, with two exceptions,[‡] and may be deemed fairly representative of the character of the Old Charges of British Freemasons.

We have likewise, reprinted " Dowland's MS." from the Gentleman's Magazine ; and lastly, we have inserted an excellent Translation from the German, by Mr. F. Berridge, (British Museum) of

---

[†] Excepting Robert's Edition of A.D. 1722, which, we believe to be a transcript of " Harleian MS. 1942,"

[‡] Viz., " Halliwell's " and " Cooke's " MSS.

(Z.) "KRAUSE'S MS.," *Printed* A.D. 1810.

It seems that this so called "York MS. of 926" was translated into Latin, and certified by "*Stonehouse*, York, January 4, 1806," after comparison with the original in the possession of an architectural Society in that city. It was subsequently translated into German by Bro. Schneider, of Altenburg, in 1808, declared to be a faithful reproduction by three Linguists, and certified to that effect by C. E. Weller, Sec. of the Tribunal of Saxony, Jany. 9th, 1809. At least, so we are told by Bro. Krause in his "Kunsturkunder der Freimaurer" (A.D. 1810, Dresden) who states that the document is an original Ancient York Constitution of A.D. 926. Strange to say however, (a) the *original* cannot be found, (b) has never been noticed in any Records of the Grand Lodge of *all* England held at York, (so far as we can discover) or (c) in the "Fabric Rolls of York Minster." (d) Bro. Drake, the Antiquary and Historian, of York, in his celebrated speech A.D. 1726 never alludes to it, (e) and it is certain that no early MS., or printed work of any kind extant in York, or in England, has yet been produced which mentions such a Constitution being, (or having been) in existence at any time. We shall not at present attempt to assist in deciding its age; but in order to give every opportunity for its examination and collation with other MSS., and early printed works like the "Polychronicon," we have decided to place it in this collection of British MSS., as it is certainly of importance, and of great value masonically, even though, it be not of A.D. 926, but, probably a compilation of the early part of the last century, like Dr. Anderson's.

———

In conclusion, we beg to express our obligations to the Brethren who have so kindly assisted in the preparation of this volume. Especially do we thank Bro. the Rev. A. F. A. Woodford, who freely placed his valuable collection of Masonic MSS. at our service, undertook to write the Preface, and, has evinced a lively interest in the progress of the work from the commencement to its completion.

We hope that the publication of these MS. Constitutions, will induce one or more competent Brethren to collate all the Copies extant, and make the result known to the Craft at an early date; for Antiquarians and Freemasons are alike interested in the subject.

Brethren And ffellowes

Here beginneth the deeds and worthy science of ffree masons
or Geomitrie and in what manner it was first ffounded and be-
-gun. And afterwards how it was confyrmed by diuers Kings
and Princes and by many other worshipfull men and
also to those that be here not inne to shew you the Charge that
belongs to euery ffree- mason to kepe ffor in good faith if you
take good hede it is well worthy to be kept for be good Craft and
curious Science. Sirs there be seuen liberall sciences of.
the which this people science of masons is one And the seauen
be these: the ffirst is Gramer and teacheth a man to speake and
writs truely the second is Rhetorice and that teacheth a man
to speake ffaire and subtill. The third is Logicke and that teach-
-eth a man to distinguish trueffrom the false. The ffourth is
Arithmeticke and that teacheth a man to reccon and chrowne
The ffifth is Geomitrie and teacheth a man Mett and measure
of Earth and of all things of the which this science is called
Mas: Crafte Geomitrie. The sixth is called Musique the seauin is
Architecture thy sixth is called Musique and doings by Vitruuius the seauin is
called Astromie and teacheth a man to know the Courss of

"DOWLAND'S MS." (W.)

THE might of the Father of Kings, with the wisdom e of his glorious Son, through the grace of the goodness of the Holy Ghost, there bene three persons in one Godheade, be with us at our beginninge, and give us grace so to governe us here in this mortall life liveinge, that wee may come to his kingdome that never shall have endinge. Amen.

Good Breetheren and Fellowes : Our purpose is to tell you how and in what manner this worthy science of Masonrye was begunne, and afterwards how it was favoured by worthy Kings and Princes, and by many other worshipfull men. And also, to those that be willinge, wee will declare the Charge that belongeth to any true Mason to keepe for in good faith, And yee, have good heede thereto ; it is well worthy to be well kept for a worthy craft and a curious science.

For there be Seaven liberall Sciences, of the which seaven it is one of them. And the names of the Seaven Scyences bene these : First is Grammere ; and it teacheth man to speake truly and write truly. And the second is Rethoricke ; and teacheth a man to speake faire in subtill termes. And the third is Dialectyke ; and teacheth a man for to discern or know truth from false. And the fourth is Arithmeticke ; and that teacheth a man for to recken and to accompte all manner of numbers. And the fifth is called Geometrie ; and that teacheth mett and measure of earth and of all other things ; of the which science is called Masonrye. And the sixt science is called Musicke ; and that teacheth a man of songe and voice, of tongue, and orgaine, harpe and trompe. And the seaventh science is called Astronomye ; and that teacheth a man the course of the sunn, moone, and starrs. These be the Seaven liberall Sciences, the which bene all founded by one Science ; that is to say Geometrie. And this may a man prove, that the science of the work is founded by Geometrie, for Geometrie teacheth a man mett and measure, ponderation and weight, of all manner of things on earth ; for there is noe man that worketh any science, but he worketh by some mett or measure, nor noe man that buyeth or selleth, but he buyeth or selleth by some measure or by some weight ; and all these is Geometrie. And these merchants and all crafts-men, and all other of the Seaven Sciences, and in especiall the plowman and tillers of all manner of grounds, graynes, seedes, vynes, plowers and sellers of other fruits ; for Grammere or Retricke, neither Astronomie nor none of all the other Seaven Sciences can noe manner find mett nor measure without Geometrie. Wherefore methinketh that the science of Geometrie is most worthy, and that findeth all other.

How that these worthy Sciences were first begonne, I shall you tell. Before Noyes floode there was a man called Lameche, as it is written in the Byble, in the iiij[th] chapter of Genesis ; and this Lameche had two wives, and the one height Ada, and that other height Sella ; by his first wife Ada he gott two sons, and that one Jahell and thother Tuball, and by that other wife Sella he gott a son and a daughter. And these four children founden the begining of all sciences

D

in the world. And this elder son Jahell found the science of Geometrie, and he departed flocks of sheepe and lambs in the field, and first wrought house of stone and tree, as is noted in the chapter above said. And his brother Tuball found the science of Musicke, songe of tonge, harpe and orgaine. And the third brother Tuball Cain found smithcraft of gold, silver, copper, iron and steele ; and the daughter found the craft of Weavinge. And these children knew well that God would take vengeance for synn, either by fire or by water ; wherefore they writt their science that they had found in two pillars of stone, that they might be found after Noyes flood. And that one stone was marble, for that would not bren with fire ; and that other stone was clepped laterns, and would not drown in noe water.

Our intent is to tell you trulie how and in what manner these stones were found, that thise sciences were written in. The great Hemarynes that was Cubys son, the which Cub was Sem's son, that was Noys son. This Hermarynes, afterwards was called Harmes, the father of wise men ; he found one of the two pillars of stone, and found the science written there, and he taught it to other men. And at the makinge of the Tower of Babylon there was Masonrye first made much of. And the Kinge of Babylon that height Nemrothe, was a mason himselfe, and loved well the science as it is said with masters of histories. And when the City of Ninyve and other citties of the East should be made, Nemrothe the Kinge of Babilon, sent thither threescore masons at the rogation of the Kinge of Nyneve his cosen. And when he sent them forth, he gave them a charge on this manner. That they should be true each of them to other, and that they should love truly together, and that they should serve their lord truly for their pay ; soe that the master may have worshipp and all that long to him. And other moe charges he gave them. And this was the first tyme that ever Masons had any charge of his science.

Moreover when Abraham and Sara his wife went into Egipt, there he taught the Seaven Scyences to the Egiptians ; and he had a worthy Scoller that height Ewclyde, and he learned right well, and was a master of all the vij Sciences liberall. And in his dayes it befell that the lord and the estates of the realme had soe many sonns that they had gotten, some by their wifes and some by other ladyes of the realm ; for that land is a hott land and a plentious of generacion. And they had not competent livelode to find with their children ; wherefore they made much care. And then the King of the land made a great Counsell and a parliament, to witt, how they might find their children honestly as gentlemen ; And they could find noe manner of good way. And then they did crye through all the realm, if their were any man that could informe them, that he should come to them, and he should be soe rewarded for his travail, that he should hold him pleased.

After that this cry was made, then came this worthy clarke Ewclyde, and said to the king and to all his great lords, " If yee will, take me your children to governe, and to teach them one of the Seaven Scyences, wherewith they may live honestly as gentlemen should, under a condicion, that yee will grant me and them a commission that I may have power to rule them after the manner that the science ought to be ruled." And that the Kinge and all his Counsell granted to him anone and sealed their commission. And then this worthy Doctor tooke to him these lord's sonns, and taught them the scyence of Geometrie in practice, for to worke in stones all manner of worthy worke that belongeth to buildinge churches, temples, castells, towres, and mannors, and all other manner of buildings ; and he gave them a charge on this manner.

The first was, that they should be true to the Kinge, and to the lord that they owe. And that they should love well together, and be true each one to other. And that they should call each other his fellowe, or else brother, and not by servant, nor his nave, nor none other foule name. And that the should deserve their paie of the lord or of the master that they serve. And that they should ordaine the wisest of them to be master of the worke, and neither for love nor great lynneage, ne ritches, ne for noe favour to lett another that hath little conning for to be master of the lord's worke, wherethrough the lord should be evill served and they ashamed. And also that they should call their governors of the worke, Master, in the time that they worke with him. And other many moe charges that longe to tell. And to all these charges he made them to sweare a great oath that men used in that time ; and ordayned them for reasonable wages, that they might live honestly by. And also that they should come and semble together every yeare once, how they might worke best to serve the lord for his profitt and to their own worshipp ; and to correct within themselves him that had trespassed against the science. And thus was the scyence grounded there ; and that worthy Mr. Ewclide gave it the name of Geometrie. And now it is called through all this land, Masonrye.

SYTHEN longe after, when the Children of Israell were coming into the Land of Beheast, that is now called amongst us, the country of Jhrlm. King DAVID began the Temple that they called *Templum D'ni*, and it is named with us the Temple of Jerusalem. And the same King DAVID loved Masons well and cherished them much, and gave them good paie. And he gave the charges, and the manners as he had learned of Egipt given by Ewclyde, and other charges moe that yee shall heare afterwards. And after the decease of Kinge DAVID, SALAMON that was DAVID'S sonn, performed out the Temple that his father begonne ; and sent after Masons into divers countries and of divers lands ; and gathered them together, so that he had fourscore thousand workers of stone, and were all named Masons. And he chose out of them three thousand that were ordayned to be maisters and governors of his worke. And furthermore there was a Kinge of another region that men called IRAM, and he loved well Kinge SOLOMON, and he gave him tymber to his worke. And he had a sonn that height AYNON, and he was a Master of Geometrie, and was chiefe Maister of all his Masons, and was Master of all his gravings and carvinge, and of all manner of Masonrye that longed to the Temple ; and this is witnessed by the Bible, *in libro Regum*, the third chapter. And this SOLOMON confirmed both charges and the manners that his father had given to Masons. And thus was that worthy Science of Masonrye confirmed in the country of Jerusalem, and in many other kingdomes.

Curious craftsmen walked about full wide into divers countryes, some because of learning more craft and cunninge, and some to teach them that had but little conynge. And soe it befell that there was one curious Mason that height MAYMUS GRECUS, that had been at the making of SOLOMON'S Temple, and he came into France, and there he taught the science of Masonrye to men of France. And there was one of the Regal lyne of Fraunce, that height CHARLES MARTELL ; and he was a man that loved well such a science, and drew to this MAMUS GRECUS that is above said, and learned of him the science, and tooke upon him the charges and manners; and afterwards by the grace of God, he was elect to be Kinge of France. And whan he was in his estate, he tooke Masons, and did helpe to make men Masons that were none; and set them to worke, and gave them both the charge and the manners and good paie, as he had learned of other Masons; and confirmed them a Chartor from yeare to yeare, to holde their semble wher they would; and cherished them right much; And thus came the science into France.

England in all this season stood voyd as for any charge of Masonrye unto St. ALBONES tyme. And in his days the Kinge of England that was a Pagan, he did wall the towne about, that is called Sainct ALBONES, And Sainct ALBONES was a worthy Knight and steward with the Kinge of his household, and had governance of the realme, and also of the makinge of the town walls; and loved well Masons and cherished them much. And he made their paie right good, standinge as the realme did; for he gave them ij, *s.*—vj, *d.* a weeke, and iij, *d.* to their nonesynches. And before that time, through all this land, a Mason took but a penny a day and his meate, till Sainct ALBONE amended it, and gave them a Chartour of the King and his Counsell for to hold a general councell, and gave it the name of Assemble; and thereat he was himselfe, and helped to make Masons, and gave them charges, as yee shall heare afterward.

Right soone after the decease of Saint ALBONE, there came divers warrs into the realme of England of divers Nations, soe that the good rule of Masonry was destroyed unto the tyme of Kinge Athelstone dayes that was a worthy Kinge of England, and brought this land into good rest and peace; and builded many great works of Abbyes and Towres, and other many divers buildings; and loved well Masons. And he had a sonn that height EDWINNE, and he loved Masons much more than his father did. And he was a great practiser in Geometry; and he drew him much to talke and to commune with Masons, and to learne of them science; and afterward for love that he had to Masons, and to the science, he was made Mason, and he gatt of the Kinge his father, a Chartour and Commission to hold every yeare once an Assemble, wher that ever they would, within the realme of England; and to correct within themselves defaults and trespasses that were done within the science. And he held himselfe an Assemble at Yorke, and there he made Masons, and gave them charges, and taught them the manners, and commanded that rule to be kept ever after, and tooke then the Chartour and Commission to keepe, and made ordinance that it should be renewed from Kinge to Kinge.

And when the Assemble was gathered he made a cry that all old Masons and young, that had any writeinge or understanding of the charges and the manners that were made before in this land, or in any other, that they should shew them forth. And when it was proved, there was founden some in Frenche, and some in Greek, and some in English and some in other languages; and the intent of them all was founden all one. And he did make a booke thereof, and how the science was founded. And he himselfe bad and commanded that it should be readd or tould, when that any Mason should be made, for to give him his Charge. And fro that day into this tyme manners of Masons have beene kept in that forme as well as men might governe it. And furthermore divers Assembles have beene put and ordayned certain charges by the best advice of Masters and fellowes. *Tunc unus ex senioribus teneat librum, ut illi vel ille ponant vel ponat manus super librum : et tunc præcepta deberent legi.*

Every man that is a Mason, take right good hede to these charges, if that any man find himselfe guilty in any of these charges, that he amend himselfe against God. And in principall, yee that been to be charged, take good heed, that yee may keepe these charges right well, for it is a great perill a man to forsweare himselfe upon a booke.

The first chaige is, that he or thou shalt be true man to God and Holy Church, and that he use neither error nor herysie by your understandinge or discreet men or wise men's teachinge. And also that he shall be true liege man to the Kinge of England without treason or any other falsehoode ; and that they know no treason ne treachery but if ye amend it privily if ye may, or else warn the Kinge or his Councell. And also ye shalbe true each one to other (that is to say) to every Mason of the science of Masonrye that bene Masons allowed, yee shall doe to them as yee would that they should doe to you ; and also that yee keep truly all the counsells of Lodge and Chamber, and all other counsells that ought to be kept by way of masonhood. And also that noe Mason shalbe in thefte or theevishe, for as farr forth as he may weete or know. And also that yee shalbe true to the lord or master that ye serve, and truly see his profitt and his advantage. And also ye shall call Masons your Brethren, or else your Fellowes, and none other foule names. And also yee shall not take your fellow's wife in villany, nor desire ungodly his daughter nor his servant, nor put him to noe disworshipp. And also that yee pay truly for your meat and drinke there yee go to borde. And also yee shall doe no villiny in that place where yee goe to bord, whereby the science might be slandered thereby. These be the charges in generall that belongeth to every true Mason to keepe, both Masters and Fellowes.

Rehearse I will now other charges singular for Masters and Fellowes. First, that noe Master shall not take upon him noe lord's worke nor none other man's worke, but hee know himselfe able and sufficient of coninge to performe and end the lord's worke, soe that the science have noe slander nor noe disworshipp, but that the lord may be well served and truly. And also that noe Master take noe worke, but that he take it reasonable, soe that the lord may be truly served with his owne good, and the Master to live honestly and to pay his fellowes truly their paie as the manner is; And also that noe maister ne fellowe shall not supplant other of their worke (that is to say) and ye have taken a worke, or else stand maister of the lord's worke, yee shall not put him out, but if he be unable of conynge for to end the worke ; And also that noe Master nor noe fellowe take noe apprentice within the tearme of seaven yeares : and that the apprentice be able, of birth freeborne, and of lymes whole as a man ought to be. And also that noe maister nor fellowe take noe allowance to be made Mason without the assent and the counsell of his fellowes at the least sixe or seaven given yeares ; and he that shalbe made Mason to be able in all manner of degrees, (that is to say) free-borne, and of good kindred come, and true and noe bondman : And also that noe Mason, shall not take noe apprentice but if he have sufficient occupacion for to occupie on two fellowes, or else three at the least ; And also that noe maister nor fellowe, put noe lord's worke to taske that was wont to goe to jornaye : And also that every Master shall give paye to his fellowes but as he may deserve, so that yee bee not deceived by false workmen : And also that none of you slander another behind his back to make him to loose his good name or his worldly goods ; And also that no fellowe within the Lodge or without mis-answer eyther ungodly or reprovably without reasonable cause. And also that every Mason shall rever-

E

ence his elder and and put him to worshippe ; And also that no Mason shall not be any common player at hazard or at the dice, nor at any other unlawfull playes whereby the science might be slondered ; And also that noe Mason shall not use noe lechery, nor be noe bawde, whereby the science might be slondered. And also that noe fellowe goe into the towne on nights tyme there as a lodg is of fellowes, without that he have a fellowe with him that he may beare him witnesse that he was in an honest place ; And also that every Master and fellowe shall come to th' Assemble, an it be within fifty myles about him, if he have any writeinge. And if yee have trespassed against the science, for to abide the award of the masters and fellowes, and to make them accorded if they may, and, if they may not accord them, to goe to the common law ; and also that ne maister, ne fellowe make noe molde nor squayar nor rule to noe layer, nor set noe layer within the lodge, nor without, to hew noe molde stones. And also that every Mason receive and cherish strange fellowes when they come over the countryes, and set them a worke and they will, as the manner is, (that is to say) yf to have no mould stones in his place, he shall refresh him with money into the next lodge. And also that every Mason shall truly serve the lorde for his paie, and every master truly make an end of his worke, be it taske or jorney, if yee have your covenants and all that yee ought for to have. These charges that wee now rehearsed to you and to all other that belongeth to Masons yee shall keepe soe helpe your God, and your holydome, and by this booke unto your power. Amen !

(Reprinted from the Gentleman's Magazine, A.D. 1815.)

"LANSDOWNE MS." (C)

About A.D. 1560.

" HERE BEGINETH THE TRUE ORDER OF MASONRIE.

" *The* might of the *Father* of the *Heavens* The *Wisdome* of the *Glorious Son*, And the goodnesse of the *Holy Ghost* three persons and one *God* be with vs now and ever *Amen.*

" Good Bretheren and Fellows our purpose is to shew you how and in what manner this *Noble* and *Worthy Craft* of *Masonry* was first founded and begun, And afterwards how it was confirmed by worthy *Kings* and *Princes* and by many other Worshipfull men, And also to all those the be heere, Weeminde to shewe you the Charge that belongs to every trew *Mason* to keep. for in good Faith if you take good heed it is well worthy to be kept for A worthy Craft and curious *Science*. *Sʳᵃ* there be *Seaven Liberall Sciencies* of which the *Noble* Craft of *Masonry* is one, And the Seaven be these, The first is *Gramer* and that teacheth A man to Spell and Write trewly, The second is *Rethorick* and that teacheth A man to speake faire and Subtill, The third is *Lodgick* and that teacheth A man deserne the trew from the false, The ffowrth is *Arethmatick* and that teacheth A man to Reckon and Account all manner of Accompts, the fifth is *Geometry* and that teacheth A man†   and Measur of Earth and of all things of the which this Science is called *Geometry*, The sixth is called *Musick*, and that teacheth A man to sing with Voyce and Tongue and Organ Harp and Trump, The Seaventh is called *Astronemy* and that teacheth A man to know the Course of the Sunn and the Moone and the Starrs, these be the Seaven *Liberall Sciencies* of the which all be founded by one which is *Geometry*, and thus a man, may prove that all the Seaven Sciencies be founde by Geometrie for it Teacheth A man†   and Measure Ponderation weight on all things on Earth, For there is noe Workman that Worketh any Craft but he worketh by some Mett or Measure. And every man that buyeth or Selleth they buy or Sell by some weight or Measure, And all this is *Geometry*, And the Merchants and all other Craftsmen of the Seaven Sciencies, and the Plowmen and Tillers of the Earth and Sowers of all manner of Graines Seeds and Vine plants, and Setters of all manner of ffruits : For *Gramer* or *Arethmatick* nor *Astronomy* nor none of all the Seaven Sciencies can no man finde Mett or Measure in without *Geometry* wherefore methinks that the said Science of *Geometry* is most worthy, And all the other be founded by it, But how this worthy Science and Craft was first founded and begun I shall tell you before *Noyes* fflood there was A man which was called *Lameth* as it is written in the Bible in the 4th Chapter of Genesis, and this *Lameth* had 2 Wifes the one called *Ada* the other Sella, by the first wife *Ada* he begat a Sonne and a Daughter And these 4 Children found the begining of all these Crafts and Sciencies in the World ffor

---

† Space in MS.

the Eldest Sonne *Gabell* found the Craft of Geometry and he fed fflocks of Sheep and Lambs in the ffeild : And first wrought houses of Stone and he and his Brother *Iuball* found the Crafts of *Musick* song of mouth harp and Organs and all other Instruments. The third Brother *Iubalican* found the Smith Craft of Gold and Silver Iron and Copper and Steel, And the Daughter found the Craft of Webbing and these Children knew well that God would take vengeance for Sinn either by ffire or Water, wherefore they wrought the Scyences they had founded in 2 Pillers of Stone, that they might be found afterwards, and the one Stone was called Marble for that would not burne in the ffire, and the other Stone was called Latherne and that would not be drowned with water ; *Our* Intent is to tell you how and in what manner these Stones were found that these Sciencies was written on the *Herminerus* that was *Cubb* his Sonne, The which *Cubb. Semet.* Sonne the which Sonne was *Noaths* Sonne this same *Herminerus* was afterwards called *Armes* the ffather of the Wisemen he found one of the 2 pillers of Stone and found the Science written therein and he taught it to others, And at the makeing of the tower of *Babilon*, was *Masonrie* first made there much of, and the *King of Babilon* called Nemroth who was a Mason himselfe and loved well the rest as is said with the Masters of Stories, And when the City of *Ninevey* or the City of the *East Port* should have bin made *Nemroth* the *King of Babilon* sent thither Sixty *Masons* of his Region to the *King* of *Ninevey* his cozen, And when he sent them forth he gave them a Charge in this manner.

" *The* first was that they should be true to their *King* Lord or Master that they served and that they shoulde Ordaine the most wise and cunning man to be Master of the King or Lords worke that was amongst them, and neither for Love Riches nor favour to sett another that had little cunninge to be Master of that Worke whereby the Lord should bee ill served And the *Science* ill Defamed.

" *Secondly* that they should call the Governor of the Worke Master all the tyme they wrought with him and other many more Charges that were to long to write, and for the keeping of all those Charges he made them sware a great Oath which men vsed at that time, And ordained for them reasonable pay that they might live with honestie, and also he gave them in Charge that they should Assemble togather every yeare once to see how they might Worke best to serve the *King* or Lord for their profitt and their owne Workship, And also that they should correct within themselves those that had Trespassed against the Science or Craft, And thus was this Noble Craft first grounded there, And the worthy *Mr Ewclides* gave it the name of Geometry, And how it is called throughout all the World *Masonrie* Long after when the Children of Israell were come into the Land *Berhest* which is now called the Countrey of Jerusalem where *King David* begun the Temple that is now called *Templu Dei*, and is named with us the Temple of *Jerusalem*, and the same King David Loved Masons then right well and gave them good pay, and he gave the Charges and Manners that he learned in Egipt which were given by that worthy Doctor Ewclid and other more charges that you shall heare after wardes ; And after the decease of *King David*, then Reigned *Solloman* that was King Davids Sound and he performed out the Temple that his ffather had begun and he sent after Masons into Diverse Countreys and into Diverse Lands and he gathered them togeather so that he had 24000 Workers of Stone and were all named *Masons* and he Chosed out of them 3000 and were all ordained to be Masters, Rulers and Governors of his worke, and then was there a King of another Region which men called *Iram* and he loved well *King Solloman* and gave

him Timber to his work and he had a Sonne that was called a man that was
Master of Geometry, and was chiefe Master of all his Masonrie & of all his
Graving, Carving and all other Masonry that belonged to the Temple, this is
Witnessed in the holy Bible (in Libro Regium quarto et Tertio) and this same
Solloman Confirmed both the Charges and the Manners which his ffather had
given, And thus was the worthy Craft of *Masonrie* confirmed in that countrey of
Jerusalem And many other Regions and Kingdoms men walked into Diverse
Countreys some because of Learning to learne more Cunning, And some to
teach them that had but little Cunning, and soe it befell that there was a Curious
man named *Namas Greecious* who had beene at the makeing of Sollomans Temple
And he came from thence into France and there he taught the *Science of Masonrie*
to men of that Land and so there was one of the Royall Line of France called
Charles Marshall and he was A man that loved well the said Craft and took upon
him the Rules and Manners and after that BY THE GRACE OF GOD he was elect
to be the *King* of ffrance and when he was in his Estate he helped to make those
Masons that were now, and sett them on Work and gave them Charges and Man-
ners and good pay as he had Learned of other Masons, and Confirmed them a
Charter from yeare to yeare to hold their Assembly when they would and
Cherished them right well, and thus came this Noble craft into ffrance and England,
in that season stood void as fforagine Charge of Masons vntill St. Albanes and
St. Albans was a worthy Knight and Steward to the King of his household and
had Government of his Realme And also of the makeing of the Walls of the said
Towne, and he loved well Masons and Cherished them much and made there pay
right good for he gave them iijs vjd a week & iijd before that time all the Land a
Mason took but one penny a day and his meat till St. Albones mended it and he
gott them a Charter of the King and his Councell for to hold a Generall Councell
and gave it to name Assembly. Thereat was he himselfe and did help to make
Masons and gave them Charges as you shall heare afterwards, soone after the
Decease of St. Albones there came Diverse Warrs into England out of Diverse
Nations so that the good rule of Masons was dishired and put downe vntill the
tyme of *King Adilston* in his tyme there was a worthy King in England that
brought this Land into good rest and he builded many great workes and buildings,
therefore he loved well Masons for he had a Sonne called *Edwin* the which Loved
Masons much more then his ffather did and he was soe practized in Geometry
that he delighted much to come and talke with Masons and to Learne of them
the Craft, And after for the love he had to Masons and to the Craft, he was made
Mason at Windsor and he gott of the *King* his ffather a Charter and Commission
once every yeare to have Assembly within the Realme where they would within
England and to correct within themselves ffaults & Trespasses that weere done
as Touching the Craft, and he held them an Assembley at *Yorke* and there he made
Masons and gave them Charges and taught them the Manners, and Comands
the same to be kept ever afterwards And tooke them the Charter and Commission
to keep their Assembly and Ordained that it should be renewed from *King* to
King, and when the Assembley were gathered togeather he made a Cry that all old
Masons or young that had any Writeings or Vnderstanding of the Charges and
manners that weere made before their Lands wheresoever they were made *Masons*
that they should shew them forth, there were found some in ffrench, some in Greek
some in Hebrew and some in English, and some in other Languages, and when
they were read and over seen well the intent of them was vnderstood to be all
one, and then he caused a Booke to be made thereof how this worthy Craft of
Masonrie was first founded and he himselfe Comanded and also then caused that

F

it should be read at any tyme when it should happen any Mason or Masons to be made to give him or them their Charges, and from that time vntill this Day Manners of Masons have been kept in this Manner and forme as well as Men might Governe it and ffurthermore at diverse Assemblyes have been put and Ordained diverse Charges by the best advice of *Masters* and ffellows ('Tunc vnus ex Senioribus tentat Librum et ille ponent manam Suam Super Librum) Every man that is a Mason take good heede to these Charges, If any man finde himselfe guilty in any of these Charges we pray that he may amend himselfe or princpially for dread of *God* you that be charged take good heede that you keep all these Charges well for it is a great perill to a man to forsweare himselfe vpon a Booke.

" *The First Charge* is that you shall be true to *God* and holy Church and to vse noe Error or Heresie you vnderstanding and by wise mens teaching, also that you shall be Leige men to the *King* of England without Treason or any ffalshood and that you know noe Treason or treachery but that ye amend and give knowledge there of to the King or his Councell also that ye shall be true to one another (that is to say) every Mason of the Craft that is Mason allowed you shall doe to him as you would be done to yoʳ selfe.

" *Secondly* and ye shall keep truely all the Councell of the Lodge or of the Chamber, and all the Councell of the Lodge that ought to be kept by the way of Masonhood also that you be noe theefe nor theeves to yoʳ knowledge free that you shall be true to the *King* Lord or Master that you serve and truly to see and worke for his advantage also you shall call all Masons yoʳ ffellows or yoʳ Brethren and noe other names :

" *Fowerthly* also you shall not take yoʳ ffellows wife in Villoney nor deflowre his Daughter or Servant nor put him to disworship also you shall truely pay for yoʳ meat or drinke wheresoever you goe to Table or Board whereby the Craft or Science may be slandered, These be the charges Generall that belong to every true Masons both Masters and Fellows.

" *Now Iʳwill rehearse other Charges single for Masons Allowed.*

" *First* that noe Mason take on him noe Lords worke nor other mans but if he know himselfe well able to pforme the work soe that the Craft have noe Slander.

" *Secondly* also that noe Master take worke but that he take reasonable pay for it, soe that the Lord may be truely served and the Master to live honestly and to pay his ffellows truely also that no Master or ffellow suplant others of their worke (that is to say) if he have taken a worke or else stand Master of a worke that he shall not put him out without he be vnable of Cunninge to make an end of his Worke, alsoe that noe Master nor ffellow shall take noe Prentice for lesse than Seaven yeares and that the prentice be able of Birth that is ffree borne and of Limbs whole as a Man ought to be and that noe Mason or ffellow take no allowance to be maid Mason without the Assent of his ffellows at the least Six or Seaven, that he that he maide be able in all degrees that is free borne and of a good Kindred true and no bondsman and that he have his right Limbes as a man ought to have.

" *Thirdly* also that a Master take noe Prentice without he have Occupcon sufficient to Occupie two or three Fellows at least.

" *Fowerthly* also that noe Master or ffellow put away Lords worke to Taske that ought to be Journey worke.

" *Fiftly* also that every Master give pay to his ffellows and Servants as they may deserve so that he be not defamed with false working.

" *Sixthly* also that none Slander another behind his back to make him loose his good name.

" *Seventhly* that noe ffellow in the house or abroad answere another Vngodly or repravably without cause.

" *Eightley* also that every Master Mason reverence his elder also that a Mason be no Common player at the Dice Cards or hazard nor at any other Vnlawful playes through the which the Science and craft may be dishonerd.

" *Ninethly* also that noe Mason vse no Lechery nor have been abroad whereby the Craft may be dishonored or Slandered.

·" *Tenthly* also that no ffellow goe into the Towne by night except he have a ffellow with him who may beare record that he was in an honest place.

" *Eleventhly* also that every Master and ffellow shall come to the Assembly if it be within 50 Miles of him if he have any warning and if he have trespassed against the Craft to abide the award of the Master and ffellows.

" *Twelthly* also that every Master Mason and ffellow that have trespass'd against the Craft shall stand in Correcon of other Masters and ffellows to make hin accord and if they cannot accord to goe to the Comon Law.

" *Thirteenthly* also that a Master or ffellow make not a Moulde Stone Square nor rule to no Lowen nor Sett no Lowen worke within the Lodge nor without to no Mould Stone.

" *Fourteenthly* also that every Mason receive or cherish Strange Fellows when they come over the Countrey and sett them on work if they will worke as the Manner is (that is to say) if the Mason have any Moulde Stone in his place on worke and if he have none the Mason shall refresh him with money vnto the next Lodge.

" *Fifteenthly* also that every Mason shall truely serve his Master ffor his pay.

" *Sixteenthly* also that every Master shall truely make an end of his worke taske or Journey whethersoe it bee.

" *These* be all the Charges and Covenants that ought to be had read at the makeing of a Mason or Masons.

" *The Almighty God who have you & me in his keeping Amen.*"

———

(A certified Transcript from the British Museum.)

"YORK MS. No. 1." (D)

About A.D., 1600.

An Anagraime upon the name of Masonrie
William Kay to his friend Robᵗ Preston
vpon his Artt of Masonrie as followeth.

M Much might be said of the noble Artt	
A A Crafts thats worth estieming in e ich part	
S Sundry Nations Noobles & their Kings also	
O Oh how they sought its worth to know	} Masonrie.
N Nimrod & Solomon the wisest of all men	
R Reason saw to love this Science then	
I Ile say noe more lest by my shallow verses I	
E Endeavouring to praise should blemish Masonrie.	

THE CONSTITUTIONS OF MASONRIE.

THE might of the Father of heaven with wisedome of yᵉ blessed Sonne through
yᵉ grace of God & goodnesse of yᵉ holy ghost yᵗ be three psons in one godhead be with vs at our beginning & give vs grace soe to governe vs here in this
life yᵗ we may come to his blessing yᵗ nevʳ shall have ending : And good brethren
& fellows our purpose is to tell yᵘ how and in what manner this worty Science
of Masonrie was begun & afterwʌrd how it was found by worty Kings & Princes
& by many other Worshipfull men, And also to them yᵗ be here we will declare
yᵉ charges yᵗ belonge to every Free Mason to keep sure in good faith.   And
therefore take good heed hereto it is well worthy to be kept well for yᵗ yᵉ Science
is ancient for there be vij liberall Sciences of yᵉ wᶜʰ it is one & yᵉ names of yᵉ
seven Sciences be these.   first Grammer wᶜʰ teacheth a man to speak truly &
write truly.   And yᵉ second is Rhetoricke & teacheth a man to speak faire plaine
in subtile termes & yᵉ third is Dielectick or Lodgick yᵗ teacheth a man to discern
truth from falshood.   And yᵉ fourth is Arithmetick & that teacheth a man to reckon
& to accompt all mannʳ of numbˢ.   And yᵉ fifth is called Geomatrie & teacheth
all measurᵉ of grounds of all other things of yᵉ wᶜʰ Science is grounded Masonrie :
& yᵉ fifth Science is called Musicke & yᵗ teacheth a man yᵉ Science of Song &
violl of tongue & organ harp trumpett.   And yᵉ seventh Science is called Astronomie & yᵗ teacheth a man to know yᵉ course of yᵉ Sonne Moone & Starrs.
These be yᵉ vij liberall Sciences yᵉ wᶜʰ Seven be all grounded by one yᵗ is to say
Geometrie for by this may a man pve yᵉ Essence of worke as founded by Geometrie so Geomatrie teacheth meat measure ponderation & weight of all manner of
things on earth for there is noe man yᵗ worketh any Science but he worketh by
some measure or weight & all this is Geomatrie, & Marchants & all crafts men &

all other of yᵉ vij Sciences & espetially yᵉ plower & tiller of all manner of graines & seeds planters of vinyeards sellᵉ of fruits, for in Grammer retorick nor astronome nor in any of all yᵉ liberell Sciences can any man finde meat or measure without Geomatrie, me thinks yᵗ this Science Geomatrie is most worthy & foundeth all others. How these worty Sciences was first begotten I shall yᵘ tell viz. Before Noah flood there was a man called Lamech as is written in the Scripture in yᵉ 4ᵗʰ Chaptʳ of Genesis And this Lamech had two wives yᵉ one named Adah by whome he had two Sons yᵉ one named Jabell yᵉ other named Jubell. And his other wife was called Zillah by whome he had one sone named Tubelcaine & one daughter named Naamah & these four children founded yᵉ beginning of all yᵉ Sciences in yᵉ world viz Jabell yᵉ eldest Sone found out yᵉ Science of Geomatre he was a keepr of flocks of sheep & Lands in the Fields as it is noted in yᵉ Chaptʳ before sᵈ And his brothʳ Juball fonnd yᵉ Science of Musicke Song of Tongue harpe & organ And yᵉ third Brother Tuball Caine found yᵉ Science called Smith Craft of Gold Silvʳ Iron Coppʳ & Steele & yᵉ Daughtʳ found yᵉ ara of Weaving And these persons knowing right well yᵗ God would take vengeance for sinne either by fire or water, wherefore they writt their severall Sciences yᵗ they had found in two Pillers of stone yᵗ they might be found aftʳ Noah his Flood And yᵉ one stone was Marble because it would not burne wᵗʰ fire & yᵉ othʳ called Lternes because it would not dround wᵗʰ watʳ now our intent is to tell yᵘ how & in what manner these Stones were found in wᶜʰ these Sciences were written the ancient Hermarines was a Cube his Son yᵉ which Cub was Sem yᵗ was Noahs Son ; these Hermarines was after called yᵉ fathʳ of wise men. he found one of yᵉ two pillers of Stone & he found yᵉ Sciences written therein & he tought yᵗ to other men, And at yᵉ makeing of yᵉ Toure of Babell there was Masonrie first much esteemed of & the King of Babilon yᵗ was called Nimrod was A mason himselfe & loved well Masons & yᵗ Science as it is said amonge Masters of Histories. And when yᵉ city of Ninevie & othʳ cities of yᵉ East should be builded Nimrod yᵉ King of Babylon sent thither sy Masons at yᵉ request of yᵉ King of Ninevie his Cousen and when he sent them forth he gave them a charge on this mannʳ yᵗ they should be true each one of them to othʳ & yᵗ they should love well one anothʳ & yᵗ they should serve their Lord truly for their pay soe yᵗ yᵉ mastʳ may have pay & all that belongeth unto him & othʳ moe charges he gave them & this was yᵉ first time yᵗ ever any Masons had any charge of his Craft. Moreover Abrahaᵐ & Sarah his wife went into Egypt And there he tought yᵉ vij Sciences to yᵉ egyptians & and he had a worty Scholler named Euclide & he learned right well & was Mr. of all yᵉ vij Sciences liberall & in his dayes it befell yᵗ yᵉ Lordes & States of yᵉ Lands had soe many Sons some by their wives & some by their concubines for yᵗ land is a hott land & plentious of Genᵉation & they had not a competent p portion of estate where-with to maintaine their sᵈ Children, wherefore they tooke much care & the King of yᵗ land caused a great counsell & sumaned a parliament to consult how they mighte pvide for their children whereon they mighte live honestly as Gentlemen & they could finde noe mannʳ of good way And then they made a pclamation throughout all yᵉ Realme yᵗ if there any yᵗ could informe them therein yᵗ he should come to yᵐ & he should be well rewarded for his travaile so yᵗ he should hould himselfe sattisfied. After this p clamation was made came this worthy Clarke Euclide & said to yᵉ 𝕽𝖎𝖓𝖌 & to his 𝕹𝖔𝖇𝖑𝖊𝖘 if yᵘ will except of me to teach instruct & governe yʳ children in yᵉ vij Sciences whereby they might live honestly as Gentlemen I shall do it upon condition yᵗ you will grant me & them a Comission yᵗ I may have power to rule them after yᵉ manner yᵉ Sciences ought to be ruled wᶜʰ yᵉ King & all yᵉ Counsell granted him & Sealed yᵉ Comsssion And

G

then this worthy Doctor tooke to himselfe Lords Sonnes & tought them yᵉ Science of Geomatrie & practise to worke in Stones all manner of worthy work yᵗ belongeth to buildings Churches Temples Castles Toures mannoˢ & all manner of Buildings & gave them in Charge on this mannoʳ. First yᵗ they should be true to yᵉ Lord yᵗ they serve & yᵗ they should love well on another & yᵗ they should be true one to anothʳ & yᵗ they should call each other his Fellow or his Brother & not his Servᵗ or Knave or othʳ foule names & yᵗ they should truly deserve their pay of their Lord or yᵉ Mʳ yᵗ they serve & yᵗ they should ordaine yᵉ wisest of them to be Mʳ of yᵉ worke & neithʳ to chuse for Love nor efection nor great nor riches to sett any yᵗ hath nor sufficient Knowledge and cunning in yᵉ worke to be Mʳ of yᵉ worke whereby yᵉ Mʳ should be evill served & they disgraced or ashamed & also yᵗ they should call yᵉ govʳ nor of yᵉ worke Mʳ dureing yᵉ time yᵗ they worke with him & other more charges yᵗ is to long here to tell & to all these Charges he made them to sweare a great Oath that men used in yᵗ time & ordained for them reasonable pay or Wages yᵗ they might live honestly thereby & also yᵗ they should come & assemble themselves together once every yeare and consult how they might best worke for their Lords pſitt & their own credit & to correct within themselves him yᵗ trespassed agᵗ yᵉ Science & thus was yᵉ Science grounded there & yᵗ worthy Mʳ. Euclid was yᵉ first yᵗ gave it yᵉ name of Geomatrie the wᶜʰ is now called Masonrie throughout all this nation And after yᵗ when ye children of Israell were comd into yᵉ land of Behest which is now called among us yᵉ Countrie of Jurie King David begun yᵉ Temple yᵗ is now called Temple Dom & is named with us yᵉ Temple of Jerusalem & yᵉ sᵈ King David loved well Masons & cherished them much & he gave them good wages & he gave them both yᵉ charges & mannʳˢ as he had learned in Egypt given formerly by Euclid and other moe charges yᵗ yᵘ shall hear afterwards after yᵉ decease of King David Solomon his Son finished out yᵉ sᵈ Temple yᵗ his father had begun & he sent for Masons into divers countreys of divers Lands & gathered them together soe yᵗ he had four score thousand workers of stone & were all named Masons he chose out of them three thousand yᵗ was ordained to be Mʳˢ. & govʳnors of his worke And furthermore there was A King of anothʳ Region yᵗ men called Hieram & he loved King Sollomon well & he gave him Timbʳ to his worke And he had a Sonne named Amon & he was a Mʳ of Geomatrie & he was chief Mʳ of all his graveings, Carvings & all of his Masons & Masonrie as appeares in Scripᵉ in Librᵒ primo Regnj & Chaptʳ yᵉ 5ᵗʰ. And this Sollomon Confirmed both Charge & mannʳˢ yᵗ his Father had given to Masons & thus was yᵗ worthy Science of Masonrie confirmed in yᵗ Country of Jurie & at yᵉ City of Jerusalem And in many othʳ Kingdomes Curious Craftsmen walked abᵗ out full wide & spred themselves into divers Countryes some to Learne moe craft & cunning & some to teach them yᵗ had little skill & cunning And yᵗ befell yᵗ there was one Curious Mason called Namus Grecas yᵗ had beine at yᵉ building of Sollomons Temple & he came into France & there he taught yᵉ Science of Masonrie to men of France & there was one of Royall line of France called Charles Martall & he was a man yᵗ loved well such a Craft & he drue to this Namus Grecas above said & he learned of him yᵉ Craft & tooke upon him yᵉ charge & mannʳˢ & afᵗwards by yᵉ Providence oḟ God he was elected King of France & when he was in yᵉ Estate he tooke & helped to make men Masons wᶜʰ before were none & gave them both yᵉ charge & yᵉ mannʳˢ & good pay as he had learned of othʳ Masons & also confirmed a Chartʳ from yeare to yeare to hold their Assembly where they would And cherished them right much thus came this famous Craft into France. England in all this time stood void of Masonrie espetialy for any Charge imposed upon yᵗ Science untill St. Albons time & in his days yᵉ King of England yᵗ was then A pagan did wall yᵉ Towne of St. Albons about & St. Albons was a worthy Kᵗ & Steward of yᵉ King's Household & had Governaute of yᵉ Realme & also had yᵉ ordering of yᵉ sᵈ Town Walls & he Loved well Masons & cherished them right much & made their pay right good considering how wages & other things stood then for he gave them ijˢ—vɪᵈ a week & iijᵈ for their nonfinch & before yᵗ time through out all this Land a mason tooke but a Peny a day untill St. Albons advanced it as above sᵈ & pcured them a Chartʳ of yᵉ King & his Counsell whereby for to hold a general counsell & gave it yᵉ name of Assembly & there at he was himself & helped to make men Masons & gave them a charge as yᵘ shall here aftʳ hear. But it happened shortly after yᵉ death of St. Albone yᵗ there arose greaᵗ warrs in England wᶜʰ came out of divers nations soe that yᵉ good ordʳ of Masonrie was destroyed untill yᵉ days of King Athelston who was a worthy King of England & brought this land in good rest and peace & builded many great workes as Abbeys Tounes & othᵣ mannʳˢ ot Buildings & loved well masons & he had a Son named Edwin & he loved Masons much more then his Father & he was a great practionᵣ in Geomatrie & he delited much to talke & comune with Masons & to learn of them skill & cunning & afterward for love he bore to masons & to their Science he was made a mason & he pcured for them of yᵉ King his father a chartʳ & Commission to hold every yeare an Assembly wheresoevʳ they would within yᵉ Realm of Eng. land & to correct within themselves defaults & trespasses yᵗ were done within yᵉ craft & he himself held an Assembly at York & there he made masons & gave them the charges & taught them yᵉ manners & comanded yᵗ rule to be kept ever after & also tooke for them yᵉ charter to keep & also gave ordʳ yᵗ it should be renued from King to King. And when yᵉ Assembly was gathered together he made pclamation yᵗ all old masons or young yᵗ had any writeings or undʳstanding of yᵉ charge & yᵉ mannʳˢ concerning yᵉ sᵈ Science yᵗ were made before in this Land or any othʳ yᵗ they should bring them forth & when they had viewed & examined there found some in French, some in Greek, some in English & some in othʳ Languages & yᵉ intent & meaning of them was found all out & he had made a book thereof how yᵉ Craft was founded & he himself gave comand yᵗ it should be read or told when yᵗ any Masons should be made & to give them yᵉ Charge And from yᵗ day to this day, Manʳˢ of Masons have been kept & observed in yᵗ forme as well as men might Observe & governe it. And furthermore at divᵉse Assemblyes an Adition of certaine things in yᵉ charges ordained by yᵉ best advice of Masters & Fellows—*Tunc unus ex senioribus teneat Librum vt ille vell illi potiat vel potiant manus Sup Librum et tunc precpta deberent Legi*—Every man yᵗ is a Mason take right good heed to these Charges & if any man find himself guilty in any of these charges yᵗ he amend himselfe before God & in pticulary yee yᵗ are to be charged take good heed yᵗ yee may keep these charges right well for it is prillous & great danger for a man to forsweare himself upon yᵉ holy Scripture. The first Charge is that he or thou be true man to God & yᵉ holy church & yᵗ yᵘ use neithʳ erour nor heresie according to yoʳ own undʳstanding or discreet & wise mens teaching & also yᵗ he shall be truly lege man & bear true Allegiance to yᵉ King of England without any treason or any othʳ falshood & if they know of any treason or treachery yᵗ you amend it privily if ye may or else warne yᵉ King or his counsell of it by declareing it to yᵉ Magistrates. And alsoe yee shall be true one to anothʳ yᵗ is to say to every Mason of yᵉ Craft of Masonrie yᵗ be allowed Masons yᵘ shall doe to them as yᵘ would they should doe to yᵘ And yᵗ yᵘ keep truely all yᵉ counsell of Lodge & chamber & all other counsell yᵗ ought to be kept by way of Masonrie & also yᵗ yᵘ use noe theeverie but keep yorselves true. And also yᵘ shall be true to ye Lord or Mastʳ yᵘ serve & truly see his pfitt & advantage pmoted & furthᵣed. And also you shall call Masons yoʳ Brethren or Fellows but not any other foul name. And yᵘ shall not take in villany yoʳ Fellows wife nor unlawfully desire his daughtʳ or servᵗ nor put him to any discredit. And also yᵗ yᵘ pay truly for yoʳ meat & drink where yᵘ goe to table & yᵗ yᵘ doe not any thing whereby yᵉ craft may be Scandalized or whereby it may receive disgrace. These be yᵉ charges in generall that belongeth every Mason to keep both Mastᵣˢ & Fellows. Now come I to rehearse certain othʳ charges singularly for Mastᵣˢ & Fellows viz That noe Mʳ take upon him any Lords Work or any other mens work except he know himself to be of suficient skill & Cuning to pform & finish yᵉ same soe yᵗ yᵉ Craft thereby receive noe slander or discredit but yᵗ yᵉ Lord be wel served & have his work truly & suficiently done And also yt noe Mʳ· take any work at unreasonable rates but so Reasonably yᵗ yᵉ Lord or ownʳ may be true served wᵗʰ his own goods & yᵉ Mʳ to live honestly thereby & to pay his fellows truly their wages as yᵉ mannʳ is. And also yt no Mʳ or Fellow shall suplant anothʳ of his work yᵗ is to say if any Mʳ or Fellow have taken any work to doe & therefore stand as Mᵣ of yᵉ sᵈ work yee shall not put him out of it unless he be unable of skill & Cuning to pforme yᵉ same to yᵉ end & also yᵗ noe Mʳ or Fellow take any apprentice undʳ yᵉ terme of Seven years & yet such apʳntice suficiently able of body & sound of lymbs & also of good birth free born noe Alian but descended of a true & honest kindred & noe bondman & also yᵗ noe mason take any apʳntice unless he have suficient occupation whereon to employ two or three Fellows at yᵉ least And also yᵗ noe Mʳ or Fellow put any to take any Lords work yᵗ was wont to work Journey work And also yᵗ every Mʳ shall give wages to his Fellowes according to his worke doth deserve yᵗ he be not deceived by false work. And also yᵗ none shall slandʳ anothʳ behinde his back whereby he may loose his good name or wordly riches. Also yᵗ no fellow within yᵉ Lodge or without shall mis answer or reprove unlawfully anothʳ without cause. And also yᵗ every Mason shall reverence his Eldʳ brothʳ & put him to honour. Also yᵗ noe Mason shall be a comon player att cards or dice or any othʳ unlawfull game or games whereby yᵉ Science may be slandered & disgraced & also yᵗ noe fellow at any time goe from his fellowes of yᵉ Lodge into any towne adjoining except he have a fellow with him to witness yᵗ he was in honest place & civill company. And also yᵗ every Mʳ & fellow shall come to yᵉ Assemblie of Masons if it be within 1: mile about him if he have any warning of yᵉ same. And if he or they have trespassed or offended against yᵉ craft all such soe trespassing shall stand there at yᵉ award & Arbitration of ye Mastᵣˢ & Fellowes there & they to make them accord if they can or may & if they cannot agree them then to goe to yᵉ comon Law & also yᵗ no Mʳ or Fellow make any mould rule or square of any Layer nor set any Layer or without to hew any mould stones. And that every Mason shall cherish strange fellowes when they come out of othʳ Countreys & set them on worke if he can as yᵉ manʳ is viz. if he have no Stones nor moulds in yᵗ place he shall refresh him wᵗʰ money to suply his necesityes untill he come at yᵉ next Lodge. And also yᵗ every Mason shall pforme his work truly & not sleightily for his pay but serve his Lord truly for his wages & also yᵗ every Mʳ shall truly make an end of his work whether it be by Tax or by Jorney viz by measure or by dayes if he have his pay & all othʳ coventˢ pformed to him by yᵉ Lord of yᵉ work according to yᵉ bargaine. These Charges yᵗ we have now rehearsed to yᵘ & to all othˢ here pʳsent wᶜʰ belongeth to Masons yᵘ shall well & truly keep to yoʳ powʳ so help you God & by yᵉ contents of yᵗ booke—Amen.

(An exact Transcript of the original, by W. J. Hughan.)

"GRAND LODGE MS." (F)

A.D. 1632.

𝕿**he mighie of the Father of heaven** and yᵉ wysdome of yᵉ glorious Sonne through yᵉ grace and yᵉ goodness of yᵉ holy ghost yᵗ bee three psons in one God, be wh us at oʳ beginning and give us grace so to govrne us here in oʳ lyving that wee may come to his bliss that never shall have ending. Amen.

𝕲**ood brethren and fellowes** our purpose is to tell you howe & in what mann wise this woorthy crafti of massonrie was begun and afterwards howe yᵗ was kept by woorthy Kings and Prynces & by many other worshipfull men and also to those that bee heire we will chardge yᵉ by the chardges that longith to evy free masson to keepe, for in good faithe, and they take good heed to yᵗ, yᵗ is woorthy to be well kepte, for yᵗ is a woorthy Crafte and a curious science, for their bee seavin liberall sciences of yᵉ wʰ seavin yᵗ is one of them, and yᵉ names of yᵉ seavin sciences be these.

The first is Grammʳ and that teacheth a man to speake trewly and to write trewly.   The second is Rhetoricke and that teacheth a man to speake faier in subtill terms.   And the third is Dialecticke and that teacheth a man to deserne or knowe trueth from falsehoode.   And the fourth is Arithmeteicke, and that teaches a man to reken and to compt all mann of numbers.   And fyfte is Geometrey and that teacheth a man the mett and measure of earth and all other things. The which science is called Geometrey.   And the sixth science is called Musicke, and that teacheth a man the crafte of song and voice of tongue and organe, harpe and trompe.   And the seavinth science is called Astronomie, and that teacheth a man to knowe the course of the Sunne & of the Mone and of the Starrs.

These be the vii liberall Sciences, the wʰ vii be all found by one Science, that is to saye Geometrey.   And this maye a manne prove that the Science of the worlde is found by Geometrey, for Geometrey teaches a man to measure, ponderation, or weight of all mann of things on earthe, for there is no mann that woorketh any crafte but he woorks by some mett or by some measure.   Nor no man buyeth or sellith but by some measure or some weight, and all this is Geometrey, and all these marchants and all Crafts men, and all other of the vi Sciences, and especially the ploweman and the tillers of all mann of graine and seeds vyneplanters, and setters of other fruits, for by Grammʳ nor Arthmeteicke nor Astronomy nor none of all the vi Sciences can no man fynde mett nor measure wʰout Geometrey.   Wherfore we thinketh that the Science of Geometrey is most woorthey that findeth all others.

𝕳**ow this woortbye Science** was fyrstle begun I shall tellyⁿ.   Before Noe's fludd their was a man that was called Lamech, as yᵗ was wrytten in the Byble in the fourth chap. of genesis.   And this Lamech had two wyves, the one wyfe height Adaa, and the other height Sella.   By his first wyfe Adaa he gat twoe Soonnes, and the one heighte Jabell and the other Juball, and by the other wyfe

Sella, he begat a son and a daughter, and theise iiij children found the beginning of all the Crafts in the worlde.   And this elder soonne Jabell found the Craft of Geometrey and he deptd flocke of sheepe and lande in the field, and firste wraught houses of stone and tree (as y^t is noted in the chapter abovesaid.)   And his brother Juball found the Craft of Musicke, Song of tongue, harp and orgain.   And the third brother Tubalcain found Smights Crafte of gold silvr and copper, yron and steele.   And the daughter found the Craft of Weaving.   And these Children knew well that God woulde take vengeance for synne ether by fyer or water, wherfore they wrytten their Sciences y^t they had found in ij pyllers of stone that they might be found after Noe's fludd.   And the one stone was marble, for that will not burne with any fyre, and the other stone was called Latres for that woulde not drown in water.

Our intent is to tell you treuly howe and in what mann these stones were found that these Sciences were wrytten in.   The great Hermarines that was Cubys Sonne the w^h Cubye was Semms Sonnne, that was Noe's soonne.   This same Hermarines was afterward called Hermes the father of Wisdome, he found one of the ij pyllers of stone and found the Science wrytten thereon, and he tauhgt y^t to other men. And at the making of the tower of Babilon there was Massonry made muche of. And the Kyng of Babylon that heighte Nemroth was a Masson himself and loved well the Craft as y^t was said with masters of stories.   And when the Citte of Nynyvie and other cities of the Est should be made Nembroth King of Babylon sent thither fortie Massons at the request of the Kyng of Nynyive his cussin, and when he sent them forth he gave them a chardge in this mann.   That they should be true one to another, and that they should live truely togither, and that they should serve their Lord truely for their paye so that their M^r· may have woorship and all y^t long to him, and other moe chardges he gave them and this was the first tyme that evr any Masson had any chardge of his Crafte.

Moreover when Abraham and Sara his wife went into Egypt and there taught the vij Sciences unto the Egyptians and he had a woorthy scholler that height Ewcled and he learned right well and was a M^r· of all the vij Sciences.

And in his daies y^t befell that the Lords and the Estats of the realme had so many soonnes that they had gotten, some by their wyves and some by other ladies of the Realme, for that land ys a hot land and plenteous of genaration.

And they had no competent lyvelyhood to find their children, wherefore they made muche care.   And then the Kyng of the land made a Greate Counsell and a Parliament, viz. howe might fynde their children honestly as gentlemen, and they could find no mann good wages, and then did they throughe all the realme that yf there weare any man that could enforme them that he should come unto them, and he should be so rewarded for his travell that y^t should holde him well pleased.   After that this cry was made then came this worthy Clarke Ewkled and said to the King and to all his great Lords, if ye will take me yor children to govrn and to teach them one of the vij Sciences wherewith they maye lyve honestly as gentlemen should, under a condition that you will grant me and them that I maye have power to rule them after the mann that the Scyence ought to be ruled. And that the Kynge and all his Consell granted anon, and seayled the comission. And then this woorthy tooke to him these Lordes Sonnes and taught them this Science of Geometrey in practicke for to woorke in stones all mann of woorthy woorke that longith to buylding Churches, Temples, Castles, Towers, and Mannors and all other mann of buylding, and he gave them a charge on this mann.

The first is that they should be true to the Kyng and to the Lords that they serve, and that they should live well together, and be trewe evy one to other, and that they should calle evy other his Fellowe or els his Brother and not his servant nor his knave nor none other foule name.

And that thei should truly deserve their pay of the Lorde or the Mr. that they serve, and they should ordeinge the wysest of them to be Mr. of the woorke, and neither for love nor lynage nor riches nor favour, to sett another that has little conning to be Mr. of the Lordes woorke wherby the lorde should be evile served and they ashamed. And also that they should call ye Govner of the woorke Mr. in the tyme that they woorke wh him. And other many mo Chardgs that are long to tell.

And to all theise chardges he made them swear a great othe that men used in that tyme, and ordeyned for them reasonable paye that they might lyve honestly by. And also that they should come and assemble togither evy yere once, howe they might woorke best to serve their Lorde for his proffitt and to their own worship, and to correct whin themselves him that had trespassed against the Crafte.

And thus was the Crafte governed there. And that woorthy Clarke Ewkled gave yt the name of Geometrie, and nowe it is called through all this land Massonrey.

Sythen long after when the children of Israele weare come into the land of Behest, that is nowe called among us the Countrie of Jerusalem, King David began the Temple that is called Templi Dom, and is named with us the Temple of Jerusalem.

And this same King David loved well Massons, and cherished much, and gave them good paye, and he gave the chardges and the mannrs as he had learned in Egipt given by Eukled, and other chardges moe that ye shall heare afterward.

And after the deceass of the King David Sallomon that was King Davids Soonne performed out the Temple that his Father had begun. And he sent for Massons into dyvrs countries and dyvrs lands and gathered them togither, so that he had four score thousand workmen that were workers of stone and weare all named Massons, and he chose of them three thousand that weare ordeyned to be Maisters and Govners of his woorke. And furthermore theare was a Kinge of another reigne that men called Iram and he loved well King Sallomon and he gave him tymber to his woorke. And he had a soone that height Aynone and he was a Mr. of Geometrey and was chief maister of all his Massons and was Mr. of all his Graving and Carving and all other mann of Massonreye that belongeth to the Temple. And this is wytnessed in the Byble in the iiij of Kyngs and thirde chapter.

And the Sallomon confirmed both Chardges and Mann that his Father had given to Massons. And thus was that woorthy Crafte of Massonry confirmed in the country of Jerusalem, and in many other Kingdoms.

Curious craftes men walked about full wyde in dyvrs countries, some to learne more crafte and couninge, and some to teache them that had bvt little couning and so yt befell that their was a curious Masson that height Naymus Grecus that had byn at the making of Sallomon's Temple, and he came into France, and there he taught the science of Massonrey to men of France. And there was one of the Royall line of France that neight Charles Martell, and he was a man that loved well suche a Crafte and drewe to this Naymus Grecus and learned of him the

Crafte and—upon him the Charges and the Mannrs. And afterwards by the grace of God he was elect to be Kyng of France.

And when he was in his estate he tooke Massons and did healp to make men Massons y^t weare non, and sett them to woorke, and gave them bothe the Chardge and mann and gave them good paye that he had learned of other Massons, and confirmed them a chapter from yere to yere to hold their Assembly where they woulde and Cherished them right muche and thus came the Craft into France.

England in all this season stode voyde of any chardge of Massonrie untill St. Albon's tyme, and in his dayes the Kyng of England that was a pagnyn he did wall thee towne aboute that is called St. Albons. And St. Albon was a woorthy Knyght and Steward to the Kyngs household and had the goument of thee Realme and also of thee towne walls, and loved Massons well and cherished them muche and he made their paye right good (standing as the Relme did) for gave them ijs and vid a weeke and three pence to their cheire, for before that tyme through all the Land a Mason toke but a peny a daye and his meat untill St. Albon amended y^t

And he gave them a Charter of thee Kynge and his counsell for to houlde a Genrall Counsell and gave y^t the name of an Assemblye, and was there at him selfe and healped for to make Massons, and gave the Chardges as yee shall heare afterwards.

Right soon after the decease of Saynte Albon thre came dyvers menes into England of dyers nations, so that the good rule of Massonry was destroyed untill the tyme of Knigte Athelstone that was a woorthy King of England, and brought all this Land into rest and peace, and buylded many greate workes of abeys and Towers and many other buyldings. And he loved well Massons, and had a sonne that height Edwin, and he loved Massons muche more than his Father did, and he was a greate practyser of Geometry, and he drew him muche to talke and comen w^h massons to learne of them the Craft, and afterwards for love that he had to Massons and to the Craft he was made a Masson. And he got of the Kyng his father a Charter and a Comission to houlde evy yere Assembly once a yere where they woulde w^{h}in thee Realme of England, and to correct within them faults and trespasses that were done w^{h}in the Craft. And he held himselfe an Assembly at **York,** and there he made Massons and gave them charges and taught them, and commanded that rule to be kept for evr after, and gave them the Charter and the Commission to keepe and made an ordynance that y^t should be renewed from Kyng to Kyng. and when the Assembly was gathered togither he made a crye that all old Massons or young that had any wryting or understanding of the Chardges and the Mannrs, that were made before in this Land or in any other y^t they should bring and shewe them. And when y^t was proved, there was founde some in Freanche, some in Greeke and some in English, and some in other languages, and they were all to one intent. And he make a booke thereof howe ye Craft was founde, and he himselfe bade and commanded that y^t should be redd or told when any Masson should be made, and for to give his Chardges.

And from that daye untill this tyme Mann of Masons have byn kept in that forme as well as men might govern y^t. Furtharmore at dyrs Assemblies certain Chardges have byn made and ordeyned by the best advice of M^{rs} and Fellowes. Tunc unus ex senioribus tenent librum, et ille vel illi opponunt manut sub libri, et tunc precepta deberent legi &. Every man that is a Masson take right good heed to those Charges yf that any fynde himselfe gylty in any of these Chardges that he may amend himself agaynste Gode. And especially ye that are to be chardged take good heede that yee keepe these Chardges right well for yt is great perill, a man to forsware himselfe upon a booke.

The fyrste Chardge y⁸ this. That ye shall be trewe men to God and holly Churche, and that yee use nor error nor heresye by yʳ understanding or discretion, but be ye discreet men or wyse men in eache thing. And also that ye should be leidge men to the King of England, without treason or any other falsehood, and that ye knowe no treason nor treechery but yᵗ ye amend freelyie if you maye, or else warne the Kyng or his Counsell thereof.

And also ye shall be true eache one to another, that is to saye to evy Mason of the Craft of Massonry that be Massons allowed ye shall doe unto them as ye would that they should do unto you. And also that you kepe all the Counsells of yʳ Fellowes truely, be yt in Lodge or in Chamber, and all other councells that ought to be keept by the waye of Masonhoode. And also that no Masson shall be a thiefe in compayne so far forth as he maye witt or knowe, and that he shall be true eache one to other, and to the Lord or Mʳ that he serve, and truely to see to his profits and to his vantadge.

And also you shall call Massons yʳ Fellowes or Brethren and none other foule names. And also you shall not take yʳ Fellowes weif in vyllany nor desyre ungodly his daughter, nor his servant put him to no diswoorship. And also that ye pay trewly for his meate and drynke there wheare you goe to boorde, and also yᵉ shall doe no villany in that place where you goe to boorde, whereby the Crafte might be slandered. These be the Chardges in generall that longth to evy Freemason to keepe both Mʳˢ and Fellowes.

Rehearse, I will other Chardges singular for Mʳˢ and Fellowes. First that no Mʳ or Fellowe take upon him any Lords woorke, nor any other mans woorke unless he knowe himselfe able and sufficient of cunning to performe the same, so that their Craft have no slander or disworshippe therby, but that the Lord maye be well and truely served. And that no Mʳ take no worke, but yᵗ he take yt reasonable, so that the Lorde maye be well served wᵗ his owne good, and the Mʳ to lyve honestly, and to paye his Fellowes trewly their paye as the mann. is. And also that no Mʳ nor Fellow shall not supplant any other of their woorke, that is to saye yf he have taken a worke in hand, or els stand Mʳ of the Lordes worke. He shall not put him out, except he shall be unable of cuning to end the work. **And also** that no Mʳ or Fellowe take no prentice but for thee terme of vij yeres, and the apprentice be able of byrthe, that is to saye free born and of lymes as a man ought to be. And also that no Mʳ nor Fellowes take no allowance to be made Masson, without Counscell of his Fellowes, and that he take him for no lesse tyme then vi or vij yeres, and that he which shall be made a Masson be able in all mann degrees, that is to saye free born, come of good kyndred, true and no bond man. And also that he have his right lymes a man ought to have.

Also that no man take any prentice unless he have sufficient occupation for to sett him on, or to sett iii of his Fellowes, or ii at the least on worke. And also that no Mʳ nor Fellowe shall take no mans woorke to taske that was wont to goe on journey. Also that every Mʳ shall give paye to his Fellowes, but as they deserve, so that he be not deceived with false workmen.

Also that noe mason slander any other behynde his back to make him lose his good name or his wordly goods. Also that no Fellow within the Lodge or without mysanswer another ungodly nor reproachfully without reasonable cause. Also that evy shall Masson reverence his elder and put him to worship. And also that no masson shall be comon player at hassard or at dyce, nor at non other unlawfull playes wherby the Craft might be slandered.

And also that no Masson shall use no leachery nor be no baude wherby the Craft might be slandered. And also that no Fellowe goe into the towne a nighte tymes without there is a Lodge of Fellowes, without he have a fellow with him that he might beare him wytness that he was in honest place. Also that evy M^r and Fellowe shall come to the Assembly, that if that it be within fyftie mylles abou^t him, yf he have any warning. And if he have trespassed against the Crafte then he to abyde the award of the M^rs and Fellowes. Also that evy M^r & Fellowe that have trespassed against the Crafte shall stand then to the award of the M^rs and Fellowee, to make them accord if they can, and if they may not accorde then to goe to the comon lawe.

Also that no Mr nor Fellowe make no mould nor square, nor rule to no layr, nor sett no layar within the Lodge nor without it to hew no moulde stones. And also that evy Mason receive and cherishe Fellowes when they come over the countreyes, and to sett them a worke, if they will, as the mann. is, that is to say if they have mould stones in his place, or els yee shall refreshe him with moony unto the next lodging.

Also that every Mason shall truely serve the Lodge for his paye, and evy M^r truly to make ane end of his worke be yt taske or journey, if he have his commands, and all that he ought to have.

"**These Charges that we have** now rehearsed unto y^u all, and all others that belong to Masons, ye shall keepe, so healpe you God, and your halydome, and by this booke in yor hands unto y^r power. Amen. So be it.
Scriptum Anno domini 1132° Die Decembris 25°

(Transcribed from the original by W. J. Hughan.)

"SLOANE MS. No. 3848" (G)

(A.D. 1646.)

THE might of yᵉ Father of Heaven, wᵗʰ yᵉ wisdome of yₑ glorious sonne; through yᵉ goodness of yᵉ holy gost; yᵗ bee three psons in one god, &c. bee wᵗʰ us at oʳ begininge; and give us grace soe to governe us in our liveinge; yᵗ wee may come to his blisse yᵗ never shall have endinge.

Good Brethren & Fellowes our purpose is to tell you, how & in what manner this Craft of Masonrie was begun, and afterwards founded by worthy Kings and Princes ⅋ many other worᵗᵗ men; and also to yᵐ that be heare; wee will declare to yᵐ the charge yᵗ doth belonge to every true Mason to keepe: For good sooth if you take heede therunto it is well Worthie to bee well kept, for a worthie Craft and curious science, For there bee seven liberall sciences, of yᵉ wᶜʰ it is one. The first is Grammer; yᵗ teacheth a man to speake truth and write truly; The second is Rethoricke yᵗ teacheth a man to speak faire ⅋ in subtill tearmes. The third Loggick, yᵗ teacheth to disearne truth from falcehood. The fourth is Arithmeticke; yᵗ teacheth to accuunt & recount all manner of numbers; The fift is called Geomeetree; and it teacheth yᵉ meate & measure of yₑ earthe; and other things, which science is Masonrie; The sixt is Musicke; wᶜʰ teacheth songe & voyce of tongue; of organs & harpe; The seaventh is called Astronomie; that teacheth to know yₑ course of sonne & moone; and other Ornaments of yₑ heavens; These 7 liberall Sciences, yᵉ which seaven bee all one Science; That is to say Geometry, Thus may a man proue, yᵗ all Science in yₑ world bee found by Geometry; for it teacheth meate and measure ponderation & waight of all manner of kind earth: And there is noe man yᵗ worketh by any Craft but hee worketh by some measure; and noe man yᵗ byes and sells, but by measure & weight, and all Geometrarians & Crafttsmen and Merchants find noe other of yᵉ Seaven Sciences; and especially Plowmen and tillars of all manner of graine; both of cornes seeds vines plaints; sellers of all other fruites; For Gramer neither Astronomie; nor any of all these can finde a man one measure or meate; wᵗʰout Geometry wherefore I thinke that science most worthy that findeth all others; How this worthy science was first begun I shall tell you; before Noes flood was a man called Lameth as it is written in yᵉ 4 Chaptʳ of Gene. and this Lameth had two wives, yᵉ one was called Adar, yₑ other Sella; and by the first wife Adar hee begott 2 sonnes. The one was called Jabell yᵉ other Juball; And by yᵉ other wife hee had a sonne & a daughter; and these foure children found yᵉ beginninge of all Craft in yₑ world; This Jabell was yᵉ elder soone; and hee found yᵉ Craft of Geomctry; and he depted flockes of Sheep & lambes in yᵉ field, And hee first wrought house of stone & tree, and it is notes in yᵉ Chapt aforesaide yᵗ his brother Juball found musicke of Songe harpe & Orgaines; The 3 Brother Tuball found out Smiths Crafts of Iron & steele; and there sister found weavinge; and these children did knowe that god would take vengencc for sinne eather by fire or water; wherefore they writ yᵉ Sciences wᶜʰ weare found in 2 pillers of stone; yᵗ yᵉ might bee found after yᵉ flood; The one stone was called marble that cannot burne wᵗʰ fire; The other was called Letera that cannot drowne wth water; Our intent is to tell you truly how & in what manner these stones weare found; where these Crafts weare written in Greeke; Hermines that was sonne to Cus; & Cus was sonne to Shem, wch was ye sonne of Naoth: The same Hermenes was afterwards Hermes; the Father of wise men and hee found out ye 2 pillers of stone where ye Sciences weare written & taught y^m forth; And at ye makeinge of ye Towre of Babilon there was the craft of Masonrie first found & made much of, ye Kinge of Babilon wch was called Hembroth or Membroth hee was a mason and loued well ye craft; as it is saide with ye maistr of ye Stories; And when ye Citie of Ninivie & other cities of East Azia should bee made. The Kinge of Babilon sent thither sixe at ye desire of the King of Ninive his cozen; and they went forth, and hee gaue h^m a Charge on this maner, That ye should bee true & liue truly together; and that ye should serue there lord truly for their payment; for that he might have worPP for sendinge y^m & other Charges hee gaue them; and this was ye first time y^t any Mason had any Charge of his Craft; Moreov^r when Abraham & Sara his wife went into Egypt there weare taught the seaven sciences unto Egyptians; And hee had a worthy Scholler called Euchild and hee Learned right well and was Maist^r of all the 7 Sciences; And it befell in his daies that ye Lords and States of ye Realme; had soe many soones y^t ye had begotten; some by there wives; & some by Ladies of the Realme; For y^t Land is a holy Land and plenished generacon; And ye had noe competent Liveige for there children; wherefore ye made much sorrowe: And ye King of ye Land made greate counsell, & a pliaint to knowe how ye might finde there Children meanes, & they could finde noe good wages; And caused a cry to bee made throughout y^e Realme; y^t if there weare any man that could informe him; y^t hee should come to him and bee well rewarded; and hold himselfe well apaide; and after this cry was made came this worthy Clarke Euchild and said to y^e Kinge and all his great Lords if you will have yo_r children govrned and taught honestly as gentlemen should bee; under condicon that you will grant y^m and mee a commission; y^t I may haue power to rule them honestly as theise Sciences ought to be ruled; and ye Kinge wth his councell granted them; & sealed y^t commission; And then y^t worthy Docter tooke the Lordes sonnes and taught y^m this Science of Geometry in practice to worke masonrie all manner of worthy workes; y^t belongeth to buildinge of castles all manner co^rts temples and churches; wth all other buildings; and hee gaue y^m charge in this manner; First that ye should bee true to ye Kinge and to y^o Lord^s ye served; & that they should love well together; and be true one to another; & that they should call one another fellowes; and not servants no knave nor other foul names; and that ye should truly serue there paymt to ye lord that others serve; and that ye should ordaine ye wisest of them to bee made M^{r.} of ye Lords worke; and neither for love great lineinge nor riches; to sett another that hath little cunninge to bee M^{r.} of ye lords worke wherebye hee should be evilly served or they ashamed; and that ye should call the govrnor of ye worke M^{r.} of ye worke whilst ye worke wth him; & many other charges which weare too long to tell; and to all these charges hee made y^m sweare the great oath men used in y^t time; and ordained for them reasonable payment; y^t ye might live by it honestly: & alsoe that y^e should come & assemble wth others that y^e might have councell in these crafts; yea might worke best to serve there lord; for his pfitt and wor^epp and to correcte themselves if y^e had trespased; and thus ye craft of Geometree was gourned there; and y^t worthy M^{r.} gave it y_e name of Geometry and it is called masonrie in this Land long after the Children of Israell were come into the land of . . . . It is now amongst us in y^e country of Jerusalem Kinge David begaun the temple of Jerusalem that is wth them templum Dei ; And y^e said King David loved masons well ; and cherished them ; and gave y^m good payment. And hee gave y^m charges that ye shall heare afterwards ; and after ye decease of King David ; Solomon y^t was sonne to King David pforned out ye Temple his Father had begun : and hee sent afterwards masons of divers Lands ; and gathered y^m together ; soe y^t hee had fourscore thousand workers of stone ; and they weare named masons ; and he had 3 thousand of them ; w^t which weare ordained M^{rs.} and Gov^{rnors} of y^t worke, and there was a King of another Region y^t men called Hyram and he loved well Kinge Solomon ; and gave him timber for his worke ; and hee had a son that was named Aynon & hee was M^{r.} of Geometry ; and he was chiefe Mr. of all his masons ; and M^{r.} of all his graued workes ; and of all other masons that belongeth to ye Temple ; & this witnesseth the Bible in libro 2. *Solo.* capite 5. And this sonne Solomon confermed both charges & manners ; y^t his father had given to masons ; and thus was ye worthy craft of masons confermed in ye country of Jerusalem ; and in many other Kingdomes Glorious Craftsmen walkeing abroade into divers Countres ; some because of learning more craft ; and other some to teach there craft ; and so it befell that a curious workman ; who was named Nimus Greacus & had beene at ye makeinge of Solomons Temple ; and came into France ; and there taught ye craft of masonrie ; to ye men of France that was named Charles Martill ; hee loved well this craft and drew to him this Ninias Greacus ; and learned of him ye craft ; and tooke upon him ye charges and mann^{rs.} and afterwardes by ye grace of god hee was elected Kinge of France ; and when hee was in his Estate hee tooke many masons ; and made masons there y^t weare none ; and sett y^m in worke and gave y^m both charges and mann^{rs.} & good payment ; wch he had learned of other masons ; and conferred y^m a charter from yeare to yeare to hold there assembly, and thus came ye craft into France ; all this while England was voyde, both of any charge or masonrie ; vntill ye time of St. Albons ; and in his time ye King of England that was a Pagan ; and hee walled ye Towne wch is now called St. Albons ; and soe in Albon's time a worthie Knight ; and chiefe Stewarde to ye King and had gou'm^t of ye Realme ; and alsoe of makinge ye Towne Walles ; and hee loved masons well ; & cherished them ; & made there paym^t right good standinge wages, as ye Realme did require. For he gave y^m every weeke iij^{s.} vj^{d.} to there double wages ; before y^t time through all ye Lan^d a masoun tooke but i^{d.} a day, and next to y^t time y^t St. Albons mended it ; hee gott y^m a charter from ye King and his councell ; and gave y^m charges as you shall heare hereafter. After ye decease of St. Albons there came greivous wars into England ; through nations ; soe y^t ye good rule of masonrie was destroyed ; untill ye time of King Athelstone ; y^t was a worthy King in England and hee brought ye Land into good rest & peace againe ; and hee builded many great workes & Castles and Abbies ; and many other Buildings ; and hee loued masons very well ; & hee had a sonne y^t was named Ladrian ; and hee loued masons much more then his Father. For hee was full of practice in Geometry ; wherefore hee drew himselfe to commune wth masons ; and to Learne of y^m ye craft ; and afterwards for ye Love hee had to masons ; and to ye craft y^t hee was made mason himselfe.

And hee gott of his Father ye King a Charter, and a commission to hold every year an Assembly where they would wthin ye Realme ; and to correcte wth y^{m.} selves statutes and trespasses ; if it weare done wthin ye crafte ; and hee held himself assembly at **York** and there hee made Masons, and gave y^m Charges and taught them the mannᵣˢ of Masons ; and Commanded that rule to bee holden evr after : And to them took yᵉ charter & Commission to keepe ; and ordained yᵗ it should be ruled from King to King : when this assembly was gathered together ; hee caused a cry to be made ; yᵗ all Masons both yong & old yᵗ had any writinge or understandinge of ye charges that weare made before in this land, or in any other Land ; yᵗ yᵉ should shew yᵐ forth and there was some in French, some in Greeke, & some in English ; and some in other Languages ; and yᵉ intent thereof was found ; & thereof hee commanded a booke to be made how yᵉ crafte was first found & made, & commanded that yₜ should bee read and told when any Masons should bee made ; and to give him his charge ; and from that time untill his time Masonrie untill this day hath beene kept in yₜ forme & ordʳ as well as men might gourne ye same ; and urthermore at dyurs assembles hath beene put to and aded certaine Charges ; more by yᵉ best advices; of Mastᵣˢ and Fellowes.

Heare followeth the worthie and godly oath of Masons. Every man that is a Masonn take Heede right well ; to this charge ; if you finde yorselfe guilty of any of these ; yᵗ you amend you ; againe especially you yᵗ are to bee charged take good heed that you may keepe this charge ; for it is a great perrill for a man to forseweare himselfe on a book.

1.   The first charge is that you shall bee true man to god ; and yᵉ holy Church ; and that you vse noe heresie nor errour by yoʳ vnderstandinge or by teaching of a discreet man.

2.   Alsoe you shall be true Leighman to the King wᵗʰout treason or falshood, and that you shall knowe noe treason, but that you amend it if you may ; or else warne the King or yᵉ Counsell thereof.

3.   Alsoe you shall bee true one to another that is to say to every Mʳ & fellowe of yᵉ trust of Masonrie ; yᵗ bee Masons allowed ; & that you doe to them as you would yᵉ should doe to you.

4.   Alsoe that no Mason bee thiefe in companie soe far forth as you shall knowe.

5.   Alsoe every Mason shall keepe true Counsell of Lodge and Chamber ; and all other Counsell that ought to bee kept by yᵉ way of Masonrie.

6.   Alsoe that you shall bee true vnto yᵉ Lorde & Mʳ that you serue ; and truly to see for his pfitt & advantage.

7.   Alsoe yᵗ you doe noe vilanie in that house whereby the Craft shall bee slandered.

These bee Charges in generall wᶜʰ every Mason should hould both Maistᵣˢ and fellowes.

Nowe I will rehearse other Charges in singular for Mʳˢ and fellowes.

1.   First that noe Maister shall take upon him any Lords worke or other worke, but that hee knowe himselfe able & cunninge to pforme the same, soe yᵗ the Craft haue noe disworpp but that ye Lord may bee serued & that truly.

2.   Alsoe that noe Maister take any worke but he take it reasonable, soe yᵗ yᵉ Lord may bee truly serued wᵗʰ his owne good ; & yᵉ Mʳ to liue honestly ; and to pay his fellowes truly there pay as the manner of yᵉ Craft doth require.

3.   Alsoe that noe Maister nor fellowe shall supplant others of there worke ; (that is to say) if yᵉ haue taken a worke, or stand Mʳ of a Lords worke you shall not put him out of it ; if hee bee able of Cunning to pforme yᵉ same.

4. Alsoe that noe M^r nor fellowe take any apprentize; to bee alowed his apprentize; but for seaven yeares; and y^t ye apprentize bee alsoe of his birth and limbs as hee ought to bee.

5. Alsoe that noe M^r nor fellowe take alowance to bee made Mason w^thout ye asent of his fellowes y^t at the least five or sixe; and that hee that shall bee made Mason; to bee able our all syers; (y^t is to say) that hee be free borne, and of good Kinred and noe bondman; and y^t hee haue his right Limes as a man ought to haue.

6. Alsoe That noe M^r put a Lordsman to taske y^t is vsed to goe to Joyrney.

7. Also every Mason shall giue noe pay to his fellowes but as hee shall diserne; soe that hee bee not deceived by falce workemen.

8. Also That noe fellowe slander other falsly behind his backe; to make him loose his good name or worldy goods.

9. Alsoe y^t noe fellowe wthin the Lodge or wthout answer another vngodlily wthout reasonable cause.

10. Also ev'ry Mason shall pferr his elder and put him to worshipp.

11. Also that noe Mason shall play at Hazards or any other unlawful game; whereby they may bee slandered.

12. Alsoe that noe Mason shall bee a common Rybold in lecherie; to make ye Craft slandered; and that noe fellowe goe into ye Towne where is a Lodge of fellowes; wthout a fellowe wth him; that may beare him witnes; that hee was in honest Companie :

13. Alsoe y^t every M^r and fellowe come to ye assembly if it bee wth in fiftie myles; about him; if hee have any warninge; and to stand at ye reward of M^{rs} and fellowes.

14. Alsoe that eu'rye Maister and fellowe if he have trespassed, shall stand at ye reward of M^{rs} & fellowes to make them acord if ye may, (but if ye may not to goe to ye Common Lawe.

15. Alsoe That noe Mason make moulds square or rule to any rough Lyers.

16. Alsoe That noe Mason sett noe layes wthin a Lodge or wthout to have mould stone wth noe mould of his owne workinge.

17. Alsoe when ye come ou^r ye country to sett them on worke as ye manner is (y^t is to say) if they have mould stones in place; he shall sett him a fortnight in worke; & giue him his hire; and if there bee noe stones for him; Then refresh him wth some money; to bring him to ye next Lodge.

18. Alsoe you shall & evruye Mason shall serue truly ye workes; and truly make an end of y^{or} workes, bee it taske or Joyrney; if you may haue y^{or} pay as you ought to haue; These Charges that we have rehearsed & all other y^t belongeth to Masonrie you shall keepe; to ye vttermost of y^{or} knowledge; Soe helpe you god & by the Contents of this booke.

Finis p me Eduardu Sankey
decimo sexto die Octobris Anno Domini 1646.

(An exact Transcript from the British Museum.)

"HARLEIAN MS. No. 1942." (M)
(About A.D. 1670.)

𝕿𝖍𝖊 𝕬𝖑𝖒𝖎𝖌𝖍𝖙𝖞 𝖋𝖆𝖙𝖍𝖊𝖗 𝖔𝖋 𝖍𝖊𝖆𝖇𝖊𝖓 with the wisdome of the glorious sonne, through the goodnes of the holy ghost, three persons in one godhead bee with our beginning, & give us grace soe to governe our Lives, that we may come to his blisse that never shall have end. Amen.

𝕲𝖔𝖔𝖉 𝕭𝖗𝖊𝖙𝖍𝖗𝖊𝖓 𝖆𝖓𝖉 𝕱𝖊𝖑𝖑𝖔𝖜𝖘.

Our purpose is to tell you how, and in what manner this craft of masonry was first began, & afterwards how it was found by worthy kings and Princes, & many other wayes hurtfull to none, & to them that bee here present, we will declare what doeth belong to every free mason to keepe ; for in good faith, if you take heed thereunto, It is worthy to bee kept, being one of the seven liberall Sciences which are these that followes.,

1st. Gramar, that teacheth a man to speak truly, and write truely.

2ndly. Rhetorick that teacheth a man to speake faire, and in subtill termes.

3rdly. Logick that teacheth a man to discerne truth from falsehood.

4thly. Arithmatick that teacheth to accompt and reckon all manner of numbers.

5thly. Geometry that teacheth met and mesure of anything, & from thence comes Masonry.

6thly. Musick that teacheth song voice.

7thly. Astronomy that teacheth to know ye course of the sunne, & moone, & other ornamts of heaven.

Note I pray you that these are found under Geometry, for it teacheth mett and measure ponderacon and weight of every thing in and upon the face of the whole earth. For you know every Craftsman works by measure, hee or shee that buyeth or selleth it is by weight or measure, husbandmen, navigators, and painters and all of them use geometry, for neither gramar, rhetorick, logick or any other of the said sciencies can subsist without geometry, *Ergo*, most worthy, laudable and honorable.

If you aske me how this science was first invented; my answer is this : That before ye generall deluge, which is commonly called Noahs flood, there was a man called Limeck, as you may read in the 4th of Genesis, whoe had twoe wives the one called Adah, the other Zillah, by Adah hee begot twoe sones Isabell and Juball, by Zillah hee had a Sonne called Tuball and a daughter called Naahmah, these fower children found ye begining of all the Craft in the world ; Jabell found out Geometry, and he divided flocks of sheepe & lands ; he first built a house of stone and timber : Juball found out Musick : Tuball found out the Smythes trade or Craft alsoe of gold, silver, copper, Iron & steele ; Naahmah found out the craft of weaving ; and these children knew well that god would take vengeance for sinne, either by fire or water, wherefore they did write these sciencies that they found in twoe pillars of stone, that they might be found after, that god had taken vengeance; the one was of marble, & would not burne, the other was Latres and would not drowne in water, soe that the one would be preserved and not consumed, if god would that any people should live upon the earth. It resteth now to tell you where these stones were found, wherein the sayd sciencies were written: After the said deluge, It pleased god that the greate Hermaxmes, whose sonne Lucium was, whoe was the sonne of Sem, whoe was the sonne of Noah, the sayd Hermaxmes was afterwards called Hermes the Father of wise men; hee found one of the twoe pillars of stone, hee found these scinces written therein, hee taught them to other men; At the tower of Babell Masonry was much made on, for the King of Babylon, whoe was Memorth was A mason, and loved the science & when the Citty of Ninneveh, and other Cittyes of the East should bee builded Nemorth sent thither threescore Masons, at the desire of the King of Ninneveh, And when they went forth, hee gave them charge after this manner.

That they should bee true one to another that hee might have worship by them in sending them to his Cozen the King: hee alsoe gave them charge, concerning theire science; and then was it, that any Mason had charge of his science; Alsoe Abraham and Sarah went into Egypt, & taught the Egiptians the seven liberall sciences, & hee had an Ingenious schollar called Euclides, whoe presantly learn'd the said liberall Sciences: It happened in his dayes the Lords and States of the Realme had soe many sones unlawfully begotten by other mens wives and Ladyes, that the land was burthened with them, haveing small meanes to mainteine them with all, the King understanding thereof caused a parliam^t to bee called and summoned for redress, but being numberless, that noe good could bee done wth them, hee caused proclamacon to bee made throughout the Realme; that if any man could devise any course how to mainteine them, to informe the King, & hee should bee well rewarded; whereupon Euclides came to the King, and said thus; my noble Sovereign, if I may have order and governmt of these L^{ds} sonnes, I will teach them the seven Liberall Sciences, whereby they may live honestly like gentlemen; provided that you will graunt mee power over them by virtue of youre Commission, which was easily effected; And the Master Euclides gave them these following admonicons.

1st. to bee true to the King.

2dly. to the master they serve.

3^{rdly}. to bee true one to another.

4^{thly}. not to miscall one another, as knave or such like.

5^{thly}. to do theire worke duely, that they may deserve theire wages at theire masters hands.

6^{thly}. to ordeine the wisest of them master, & theire Lord and Master of his work.

7^{thly}. to have such reasonable wages, that the workmen may live honestly with creditt.

8^{thly}. to come and assemble once a year to take Counsell in theire Craft how they may worke best to serve theire Lord and Master for his proffit and theire owne credit and to correct such as have offended;

Note that Masonry was heretofore termed Geometry, & since then the people of Israell came to the land of Behest, which is now called Emens, in the Country of Jerusalem, King David began a Temple, which is now called the Temple of the Lord, or the Temple of Jerusalem, and King David loved Masons well, and

I

cherished them and gave them good paym^t and did give them a charge as Euclides have given them before in Egipt, and further as hereafter followes.

And after the death of King David Solomon his sonne finished the Temple, which his Father began hee sent for Masons of divers Lands, to the number of fower and twenty thousand, elected and nominated Masters and Governos of the work, & there was another King of another Religion or Country called Haram, whoe loved well King Solomon, & hee gave him timber for his work, and hee had a sonne Anon & hee was master of Geometry, & hee was cheife Master of all his Masons, of Carved work, and all other theire work of Masonry, that belongeth to the Temple, as appeareth by the Bible, in libro Regum Cap: 4to & King Solomon confirmed all things concerning Masons, that David his father had given in charge, & these Masons, did travell divers Countrys some to augment theire knowledge in the said Art, & to instruct others ; And it happened that a curions Mason called Memon Grecus, that had beene at the building Solomons Temple, came into Fraunce, & taught the Science of Masonry to the French men, & there was a King of Fraunce named Carolus Morter, whoe loved greatly Masonry, which sent for this said Memon Grecus, & learned of him the sayd Science, & became of the Fraternity, therefore hee began great works, & liberally did pay his workmen, & confirmed them a large charter, and was yearely present at theire assembly, which was a greate honour, and encouragem^t to them, & thus came the Science into Fraunce ; Masonry was unknown in England untill St. Alban came thither, whoe instructed the King in the said Science of Masonry, As alsoe in Divinity, whoe was a Pagan ; hee walled the towne called St. Albanes, hee became in favour with the King, insomuch that he was knighted and made the Kings cheife Stewards, & the relame was govern^d by him under the King, & hee greatly cherished, and loved Masonry, and truely paid them theire wages weekly, which was 3$^s.$ 6$^d.$ p weeke, he purchased them a large Charter from the King, to hold a general^{ll} assembly and Counsell yearly ; hee made many Masons, & gave them such a Charge, as is hereafter declared, It happened presently after the martirdome of St. Alban, whoe is truely termed England's proto Martyr, that a certaine King invaded the land, & destroyed most part of the natives with fire & sword that the science of Masonry was much decayed untill the Reigne of King Athelstone, which some writ Adlestone, whoe brought the land to peace and rest from the insulting Danes ; hee began to build many abbyes, monasteryes, & other religious houses, as alsoe Castles, & other tresses for defence of his Realme ; hee loved Masons more then his Father ; hee greatly studdyed Geometry & sent into many lands, for men expert in the Science ; hee gave them a very large charter, to hold a yearely Assembly to correct offenders in the sayd Science, & the King himselfe caused a generall assembly of all Masons in the Realme at 𝔜𝔬𝔯𝔨 & there made many Masons, & gave them a deepe charge for observacon of such Articles as belonge to Masonry, and delivered them the said Charter to keepe, & when his Assembly was gathered together, hee caused a cry to bee made, that if any Mason of them, had a writing that did concerne Masonry, or could Informe the King, in anything, or matter, that was wanting in the said Science, already delivered, that they, or hee, should deliver them to the King, or write them to him, And there were some in French, some in Greek, some in English, and other Languages whereupon the King caused a book to bee made, which declared how the Science was first invented & the utility thereof, which book he commded to bee read, and plainely declared, when a man was to bee made Mason, that he might fully understand what Articles, Rules, and Orders he was obliged to observe, & from that time untill this day;

Masonry hath been much respected and preserved, & divers new Articles hath been added to the sayd charge, by good advice and consent of the best Masons and Fellowes.

Tunc unas ex senioribus teneat librum illi qui jusjurandu reddat et ponat manum libro vel sup librum, dum Articulum et precepta sibi legantur.

Say thus, by the way of exhortacon, my loveing and respective friends, and brethren, I humbly beseech you, as you love your souls eternal wellfare, yo$_r$ owne credit, & youre countryes good, bee very carefull in observacon of these articles that I am about to read to this Depon^t for you are oblieged to pforme them as well as hee, soe hopeing of y^r care herein I will (by god's grace) begin the charge, I am to admonish you to hono^r god, & and his holy church; that you use noe heresie or error in your understanding or discredit men teaching.

2dly. I am to admonish you, to bee true to our Sovereigne Lorde the King, committing noe treason, misprision of treason, or felony, & if any one shall commit treason, y^t you know of, you shall give notice to his Mat^{ie} his privy Counsellors or some other that have commission to enquire thereof.

3dly. You shal bee true to youre fellows and brethren of the Science of Masonry, & doe to them as you would bee done unto.

4^{thly}. If you shall secure and keepe secret the obscure and intricate parts of the Science, not disclosing them to any but such as study & use the same.

5^{thly}. You shall doe youre work truely, & faithfully endeavouring the profitt and advantage of him, that is owner of the sayd work.

6^{thly}. You shall call Masons, fellow or brethren, without addicon of knave, or any other bad Language.

7^{thly}. You shall not take your neighbours wife villaniously, nor his da nor his mayd to use ungodlily.

8^{thly}. You shall not carnally lye with any woman, belonging to the house wherein you are at table.

9^{thly}. You shall truely pay for youre meate & drink where you are at table.

10^{thly}. You shall not undertake any mans work knowing yourselfe unable and unexpert to pforme and effect the same.

That noe aspercon or discredit be imputed to the science or the L^d or owner of ye same work be any wayes prejudiced.

11^{thly}. You shall not take any worke to doe at any excessive & unreasonable rates, or deceive the owner thereof, but soe as he may be truely, and faithfully served with his owne goods.

12^{thly}. You shall not supplant any of youre fellows of theire work (That is to say) If he, or they, or any of them, have taken any work upon him, or them, or they stands Masters of Lords or owners work, that you shall not put him or them out of or from the said work, although you pceive him or they unable to finish the s$_d$ work.

14^{thly}. You shall not take any apprentice to serve you in the sayd Science of Masonry under the terme of seven yeares, nor any but such as are descended of of good parentage, that noe scandall may bee imputed to the Science of Masonry.

15^{thly}. You shall not take upon you to make any one mason without the privity and consent of five or six of your fellows, & none but such as one that is free borne, & whose parents live in good fame, & name & that hath his right and pfect limbes, and psonall of body to attend the said Science.

16^{thly}. You shall not pay any of youre fellowes more money, than hee, or they have deserved, that you be not deceived by false or by slight working, and and the owner thereof much wronged.

17^{thly}. You shall not slander any of youre fellows behinde theire back to impaire temporall estate or good name.

18^{thly}. You shall not without urgent cause answer yor fellow doggedly or ungodlily, but as becometh a loveing brother of the same Science.

19^{thly}. You shall duely reverence, youre fellow, that the bond of Charity and mutuall Love may continue steadfast and stable amongst you.

20^{thly}. You shall not (except in Christmas time) use any unlawfull games, as Cards, Dice, &c.

21^{stly}. You shall not frequent any house of Bawdry or bee a pawnder to any of youre fellowes, or others, which wilbee a greate scandall to the Science ; You shall not goe out to drink by night, or if occasion doe happen that you must goe, you shall not stay till past eight of the clock, haveing some of youre fellowes, or one at the least, to have you witness of the honest place you were in, and your good behaviour to avoid scandall.

22^{ndly}: You shall come to the yearely assembly, if you know where it is, being within tenne miles of the place of youre abode ; submitting yourselfe to youre fellows, wherein you have erred, to make satisfaction, or to defend by order of the kings laws.

23^{rdly}. You shall not make any mould square or rule to mould stones wthall but as such is allowed by the fraternity.

24^{thly}. You shall set strangers at work, having Imploymt for them, at least a fortnight & truely pay them theire wages ; and if you want work for them, you shall relieve them with money to defray theire reasonable charges to the next Lodge.

25^{thly}. You shall truely attend youre work, & truely end the same, whether it bee taske or Journey worke, if you have youre wages and paymt truely.

These Articles and Charge which I have rehersed to you, you shall well and truely, observe & keepe to your power, soe helpe your god, and the contents of this booke.

𝕿𝖍𝖊 𝕹𝖊𝖜 𝕬𝖗𝖙𝖎𝖈𝖑𝖊𝖘.

26 : Noe person (of what degree soever) bee accepted a free Mason, unless hee shall have a lodge of five free Masons ; at least, whereof one to bee a master, or warden, of that limitt, or devision, wherein such Lodge shalbee kept, & another of the trade of Free Masonry.

27 : That noe *p*son shal bee accepted a Free Mason, but such as are of able body, honest parentage, good reputacon & observers of the Laws of the Land.

28 : That noe *p*son hereafter bee accepted free Mason nor shalbee admitted into any Lodge or assembly untill hee hath brought a Certificate of the time of accepcon from the Lodge, y^t accepted him, unto the Master of that Limit, &

Division, where such Lodge was kept, which sayd Master shall enrole the same in parchmt in a role to bee kept for that purpose, to give an acct of all such acceptions at every generall Assembly.

29 : That every person whoe now is Free Mason, shall bring to the Master a note of the time of his acception to the end the same may bee enrolld in such priority of place of the *p*son shall deserve, & to ye end the whole company and fellows may the better know each other.

30 : That for the future the sayd Society, Company, & fraternity of Free Masons shalbee regulated, & governed by one master, & Assembly, & Wardens, as ye said Company shall think fit to chose, at every yearely generall Assembly.

31 ; That noe *p*son shalbee accepted a Free Mason or know the secrets of the said Society, untill hee hath first taken the oath of secrecy hereafter following.

I, A. B., Doe in the presence of Almighty God, & my Fellowes, & Brethren, here present, promise and declare, that I will not at any time hereafter, by any Act or circumstance whatsoever, Directly or Indirectly, publish, discover, reveale, or make knowne any of the secrets, priviledges, or Counsells, of the Fraternity or fellowship of Free Masonry, which at this time, or any time hereafter, shalbee made knowne unto mee, soe helpe mee God, & the holy contents of this booke.

1.   You shall truely honour God, & his holy Church, The King, youre Master, & Dame, you shall not absent yourselfe but with the License of both or one of them, from theire service, by day or night.

2.   You shall not purloyne or steale, or bee privy or accessory to the purloyning or stealeing to the value of sixpence, from them, or any of them.

3.   You shall not comit adultery or fornicacon in ye house of youre Master, with his wife, daughter or mayd.

4.   You shall not disclose youre Master or Dame theire Counsell or secrets, which they have imputed to you, or what is to be concealed, spoken or done, within the precincts of theire house, by them, or either of them, or any Free Mason.

6,   You shall reverently behave yourselfe to all free Masons, not using Cards, or Dice, or any other unlawfull Games, (Christmas excepted.)

7.   You shall not haunt or frequent any Taverns, Alehouses, or such as goe into any of them except upon your Masters, or Dame, theire or any of theire affaires, or without theire or any of their consent.

8.   You shall not comit Adultery or Fornicacon in any Mans house, where you shall bee at table or at work.

9.   You shall not marry or contract yourselfe to any woeman during youre Apprenticeshipp.

10.   You shall not steale any mans goods, but especially yor sayd Masters, or any of his Fellow Masons, or suffer any one to steale of theire goods, but shall hinder the Fellow if you can, if you cannot, then you shall acquaint your sayd Master & his fellows presantly.   Finis.

(Transcribed from the original in the British Museum.)

"LODGE OF HOPE MS." (N)

(About A.D. 1680.)

THE Constitutions Articles which are to be observed and fulfiled by al those who are made free by the R^t Worl, Mrs. Fellowes and Brethren of Free Masons at any Lodge or Assemblie.

𝕿𝖍𝖊 𝖒𝖎𝖌𝖍𝖙 𝖔𝖋 𝖙𝖍𝖊 𝖋𝖆𝖙𝖍𝖊𝖗 𝖔𝖋 𝖍𝖊𝖆𝖇𝖊𝖓 and the wisdom of his gracious Son through the goodness of the holy ghost. viz. three persons and one god be with us at the beginning and give us grace soe to govern our lives ; that we may come to Eternal Joy. Amen.

𝕲𝖔𝖔𝖉 𝕭𝖗𝖊𝖙𝖍𝖗𝖊𝖓 𝖆𝖓𝖉 𝖋𝖊𝖑𝖑𝖔𝖜𝖊𝖘 our purpose is to relate unto you how, and in what manner the Craft of Masonry was at the first begun and afterwards how it was found out by mighty Kings and whereby Princes and many other worshipful men and also to them that be heare will declare the charge that belongs to every true Mason to keep; for in good faith if you take heed thereunto, it is well worthy to be kept for a worthy craft, and a curious science for their be Seaven liberall Sciences of the which it is one of these following

The first is Gramer that teacheth a man to speake, the Second is Logicke y^t teacheth to decerne the truth from falshood. The Third is Rhetorick that teacheth to speake and in Subtilly tearms : The fourth is Music that teacheth the art of Song and the Voice of Organs and Harps ; The fifth is Aretmaticke that teacheth to account and reckon all maners of Numbers. The Sixth is Geometry that teacheth to measure ye Earth and other things of which Science is Masonry, The Seaventh and last is called Astrology or Astronomy that teacheth to know the course of the Sun and Moon & other Ornaments of the Heavens.

The Seaven liberal Sciences which be all by one Science viz : Geometry it teacheth Mett and Measure ponderation and weight of all manner of things in the Earth and there is noe man worketh by any Craft but he worketh by some Measure, and all is Geometry Craftsmen and Merchants depend upon this Science & Especially plowmen and tillers of ground both for Corne and Seed and Vines and plants flowers & other fruite of the Earth, for neither Gramer nor Astronomy nor any of the rest doe find a man one Measure without Geomtry, Wherefore that Science is most worthy that findeth all other ; how that this Science was first begun I shall tell you

Before Nohas flood was a man called Lamech had two wives the name of the one was Adah and the other Sella as it is written in Genises 4th Chapter ; by the first wife Adah, he begott four Sonnes the one was called Jaball, and the other Juball, and by the other wife he had a Sonn called Tuball Cain and a daughter called Naamah and these children found the beginning of all Crafts and Sciencs in the world, thus Jabell was the elder and found out Geometry, and parted flocks of Sheep and Lambs in the field, and first wrought house of Stone & tree as it is written in the chapter aforesaid v. 21. and his brother Juball found out Musicke of Song Harps and Organs, and the third brother found out the Smith Craft as of Iron or Steel and there Sister found out the Craft of weaving, these children did know that God would take Vengeance for Sin, either by fire or water wherefore they wrote the Sciences, which they had invented in two pillers of Stone, that they might be found after the flood, the one stone is called Marble which cannot burne with fire, and the other Stone is called Laternus that will not drowne in water.

The great Hermerinus that was Sonne unto Guz and Guz was Sonn unto Ham which was son unto Noah, the Second Sonne Hermerinus was after called Hermes the father of Wisdome, and he found out the two pillars of Stone, and the Sciences written therein he taught, and at the buildinge of the Tower of Babilon was called Nembroth. Nemrod was a Mason and loved well the Craft, and it is said by the Masters of the Stone y^t when the City of Nineve and other Cityes should be builded Nembroth the King of Babilon sent their Sixty Masons, att the desire of the King of Nineve his Couzen and when they went forth he gave them a charge on this manner viz—That they should be true, and to love one another ; and that they should serve truely the lord for his payment that he might have worship by sending of them unto him, and other things he gave them in Charge and this was the first time that the Masons had any charge of their Craft, Moreover when Abraham and Sarah his Wife went into Egypt, and there they taught the Seaven Sciences to the Egyptians. They had a worthy Scholer called Euclides and served right well ; and was Master of all the Seaven Sciences, and it befell in his dayes that the Lords and States in the Land had soe many Sonnes that they had begotten some by their wives and some by other Ladies of the realme (for that land was holden a plenished generation) and noe living competent for there said children wherefore they were sore troubled in minde, in what sort to puide for them : And the King of that land made a great Counsell and a parliament to know how they may find there children, and he could noe way that was goud ; bnt caused a proclamation to be made through the realme if their were any man could informe them that he should come to him, and he should be rewarded for his travell ; and hold himselfe well pleased, after the cry or proclamation was made, came the worthy clarke Euclides, and said to the king and all the great lords if you will give me your children to govern and teach honestly as gentlemen should under condition that you will grant them and me a Commission that I have to rule honestly, as that Science ought to be used and ruled ; and the King granted anon, and sealled a Commission and then the worthy Doctor took the lords sonns and taught them the Science of Geometry for to worke in Stones all manner of worthy work that did belong to Castles and all manner of Courts Temples, and all manner of Churches, with all other buildings, and he gave them a Charge in this manner, First that they should be true to the King and the Lord whom they served and they should be true one to another and they should call each other felow and not servant, nor knave nor any other foul name and they should ordaine one of the wisest of them to be Master of the lords work, and neither for low nor great livings, nor riches to lett any that had little understanding to be Master of the lords worke ; whereby ye lord should be evil served, and they should call the governor of the work the Master of the work whilest they wrought with him, many other Charges which were long to relate, and to all other charges he made y^m to swear the great oath. that men used to swear at that time, and ordained them reasonable payment that they might live by it honestly, and also that they should come and assemble themselves, and have Councell in the Art of Geometrey governed their ; and that worthy Master gave it that name & was called Masonry in this land, long after the Children of Israel were come into the land of Beliel, it is now called amongst us ye Countrey of Jerusalem. King

David begun the temple of Jerusalem which is called with them Temple of Diana and the same King David love Masons well and cherished them and gave them payment, he gave them the Charges and manners, as he had it out of Egypt given by Euclides and other charges which you shall hear afterward, and after the death of King David, Solomon his Son performed the Temple that his father had begun and sent divers Masons of divers land, and gathered them together so that their was Eighty thousand Workers of Stone & they were named Masons and he had three thousand three hundred of them which were ordained to be Masters and governors of the work and their was a King called Hiram, and he loved King Solomon and he gave him timber for his worke, and he had a Son named Amon & he was Master of Geometry and was the Master of all his workmen (or Masons) and Master of all his graven and carved works and to all other masonry that belonged to the temple as it is written in the Bible 1 Kings fifth Chap: and the same Solomon confirmed both the charges and manners that his father had given Masons : and thus the worthy Craft of Masonry was first confirmed in the countrey of Jerusalem and in many other kingdoms glorious craftsmen walked abroad because of learning more craft, and others to teach their craft; and soe it came to passe that the curious Mason named Minus Goventis (or Grevis) that had been at the building of Solomons Temple and in France he taught ye Craft of Masonry to men in France, and their was one of ye royall line of France that was called Charles Martell he loved Minus Goventis well because of his craft, and he tooke upon him ye charges and manners and afterwards by the grace of God he was to be elected King of France, and when he was in his realme he took to him many Masons their & Manners and he ordered them good payment which he had learned of other Masons, and he confirmed them a Charter to hold from yeare to yeare & cherished them much and thus came the Craft into France. *England* all this while stood voyde of Masons untill the time of St. Albone and in his time the King of England was a pagan and builded the town yt is now called St. Albons after that in Albons time was a worthy Knt & he was chief Steward with the King and had ruleing of the realme, & also of makeing the Towne wall and he loved Masons well and cherished them much and he made their payment right standing as the realme did require for he gave them every week iiis. vid. to their double payment or wages, before yt time through all that land, a Mason took but a penny a day and afterwards St. Albone amended it much and gott them a Charter from ye King and Counsell and gave it the name of an assemblie, and theirat he was himself and made Masons and gave them a Charge as you shall hear afterwards—Right soon after the death of St. Albone came great warrs into Ingland through divers natione Soe yt good rule of Masonry could not be used untill that Athelstone who was a worthy King in England who brought the land into great peace, and builded many great buildings of Abeys and Castles and many other great buildings, and he loved Masons very much And he had a Sonn was Hoderine and he loved Masons much more than his father, for he was full of practise in Geometry wherefore he drew himself to Common Masons, and to learn their Craft and afterwards for love he had to Masons and the Craft he was made Mason himself and he gott of his father the king a Charter and Commission to hold every yeare an Assembly where they would within the realme and correct within themselves faults and tresspases that was done within the Craft, and he made himself an Assembly at 𝔜𝔬𝔯𝔨𝔢 and there he made Masons and gave ym charges and taught them manners of Masons and comanded that rule should be kept ever after and to them he gave ye Charter and Commission to keep and make ordinance, that it should be ruled from King to king when his Assembly was charged he made a Cry that all Masons that had any writeing or understanding of the craft, that were made before in his land that they should shew yᵐ forth, and their was some in french, and some in greek and latin, and some in English and other languages, and the intent theirof was found, and he comanded a booke theirof to be made how the craft was first found and comanded yᵗ it should be redd' and told where any Mason should be made, and to give him his Charge, and from that time Masons have kept in this forme, and order as well as men might govern it, and furthermore at private Assemblyes their have been added to it divers Charges more and more by the Master and fellows advices.

Tunc unus ex Senoribus teneat librum et ille vel illi ponant manus supra librum et tunc preceept debeat legi, viz :

Every man that is a Mason take heed to this Charge if you find yourselves guilty of any of these that you amend again and especially you that is to be charged take you heed yᵗ you may keep the Charge, for it is a great perill for a man to foresware himselfe on a Booke.

1 The first Article of your Charge is that you shall be true to **God and the Holy Church** that you use noe Heresie nor Eror to your understanding.

2 Alsoe you shatl be true leige men to the King without treason or falshood and that you shall know noe treason, but that you may amend it (if you may) or else warne yᵉ King or his Counsell of it.

3 Alsoe you shall be true one to another, Viz :—to every Mʳ and fellow of the Craft of Masonry yᵗ be Masons alowed, yᵗ you doe to them as you would they should doe to you, also that every Mason shall keep true lodge and Chamber ; and all other Counsell that ought to be kept by way of Masonry.

4 Alsoe you shall be true to yᵉ lord and Master, whom you serve and truly to seek his profite and advantage.

5 Alsoe you shall call Masons your fellows and brethren and noe other foule name neither shall you take your fellowes in Villany nor ungodlily his daughter or his wife in Villany.

6 Alsoe that you shall pay truely for your Table, and meat and drink where you goe to board.

7 Alsoe that you doe noe Villany in that house whereby yᵉ Craft may be slandered.

These be yᵉ charges in generall yᵗ every Mason should hold, both Masons and fellowes.

These Charges which belong onely to the Masters and fellowes.

1 That noe fellowe shall take any lords worke or other, but he know himself able and cunning to perform the same soe that yᵉ Craft have noe disworship but that yᵉ lord may be well and truly served.

K

2   Alsoe that noe Master take any worke but that he take it reasonably, soe that the lord may be served truely with his own goods, and the master to have honestly and pay his fellowes truly their pay as the manner of the craft doth require.

3   And also that no master or fellow shall suplant others viz :—if he have taken any worke or stand master of a lords worke you shall not put him out if he can finish the worke.

4   Alsoe that noe Master or fellow shall take an aprentice to be alowed his aprentice but in seaven yeares, and your aprentice to be able of his birth, and of limbs as he ought to bee.

5   Alsoe, that noe master or fellow shall take any allowance to be made Mason, without the consent of his fellowes (five or six or least).

6   Alsoe, he that shall be made Mason, shall be free born, and of good kindred, and noe bondman, and shall have his right limbs, as a man ought to have.

7   That noe M^r shall put any lords work to task, that use to goe to Journey.

8   That noe M^r shall give a penny to his fellowes, but as he deserves it, soe that he be not deceived with false workemen.

9   Alsoe, that noe fellow shall slander another behind his back to make him lose his good name or his worldly goods, and alsoe that noe fellow within the lodge or without, may answer his fellow disrespectively without a reasonable cause.

10   Noe Mason shall play at hazard or other play, whereby they may be slandered.

11   Noe mason shall be a comon riball in litchery, to make his master to be slandered.

12   Noe fellow shall goe into the Towne in the night-time, where is a lodge of fellowes without a fellow with him, that he may bear him witness, that he was in an honest house or place.

13   That every Mason or fellow come to the assembly, if it be within five miles about him : if he have warninge, and their stand at the reward of the M^{rs} and fellowes.

14   Every Mason shall prefer his fellow, and put him to worship.

15   Every M^r and fellow if he have trespassed, shall stand at reward of Masters and fellowes if he or they may make them account, and if they may not accord then to goe to the comon assembly.

16   That noe Mason shall make any Mould square or rule to any rough layer.

17   Noe mason which is within a lodge or without, shall sett or lay, Mould, Sconder, without mould of his owne makeing.

18   Every Mason shall receive strange masons or fellowes when they come over the Countery and set them in worke as the order is viz :—if he have Mold, Sconder to place, he shall sett him two weeks at the least in worke and give him his hire and if there be no Sconder, for him then to refresh him with money to bring him to the next lodge, and alsoe all masons shall be true to their work be it by taske or journey and truely make an end of their worke ; that they may have their pay as they ought to have it.

The Apprentice Charge.

That he shall be true to god, and the Holy Church, the King his master and dame whom he shall serve.

That he shall not steall or pick away his Master or Dames goodes   absent himselfe from their service, nor goe from them about his own pleasure by or by night without licence of them.

That he doe not comit Adultery or fornication in his master house with his wife daughter or servant.

He shall keep Counsell in all things spoken in lodge or chamber by Masons fellowes or free masons, and that he shall not keep any disobedient argument against any Mason nor disclose any secrett whereby any (difference) may arise amongst Masons or fellowes or apprentice, but (reverently) to behave himself to all free masons, being sworn brethren to his said Master.

He shall not use any carding, dicing or other unlawful games, haunt any Taverns or Alehouses their to waist any mans goodes without licence of his Master or some other free masons.

He Shall†

Examined and compared with the scroll this 7th day of March, 1872.

Wm. W. Barlow, W.M., 302.

----

† Here the parchment scroll is defaced, worn away with age, and torn off.

THE "ANTIQUITY MS." A.D. 1686.

In the name of the
Great and holy God

Fear	the wisdome of the Son and	For
God And	the goodnesse of the holy	This is the
Keep His	Ghost Three Persons & one	Whole Duty
Commmandments	God be with us now &	of Man
	ever. Amen.	

Bretheren and Fellowes here begineth the Noble and Worthy Science of Free Masons or Geomitrie and in what maner itt was first Founded and begun, And afterwards how itt was confirmed by diverse Kings and Princes and by many other Worshipful men and allso to those that be here we mind to shew you the Charge that belongs to every Free Mason to keepe For in good faith if you take good heed it is well worthy to be kept for A Noble Craft and curious Science. Sirs there be seaven Libreall Sciences of the which this Noble Science of Masons is one And the seaven be these.   the First is Gramer and teacheth a man to spell and write truely.   The Second is Rhetoricke and that teacheth a man to speake Faire and Subtill the Third is Logicke and that teacheth a man to descerne the truth from the False The Fouerth is Arithmeticke and that teacheth a man to reckon and Account.   The fifth is Geomitrie that teacheth a man Mett and measure ot Earth and of all things of the which this Science is called by Mastr Euclides Geomititrie and by Vitruouis is called Architecture the sixth is called Musique seaueum is called Astromie and teacheth a man to know the course of the Sun and the Moon and the Starrs These be the seaven Libreall Sciences of the which all be Founded by one that is Geomitrie and thus a man may prove that all the Seauen Sciences be Founded by Geomitrie for it teacheth a man Mett and measure Ponderaton and waight on all the things on Earth for there is no workman that worketh any Craft but he worketh by some mett or measure and every man that buyeth or selleth they buy or sell by some waight or measure and all this is Geomitrie and the Merchants and all other Craftsmen of the seaven Sciences and the Plowman and the Tillers of the Earth and the Sowers of all maner of Graines seeds vines and plants and setters of all maner of Fruits for Grammer or ARITHMETICKE nor Astronomie nor none of all the seaven Sciences can no man fine mett or measure in without Geomitrie wherefore methinks the said Science ot Geomitrie is most worthy and all the other be Founded by itt. But how this worthy Science and Craft was First Founded and begun I shall tell you—Before Noah's Flood there was a man which was called Lameth as it is written in the Bible in the 4th Chapter of Genesis and this Lameth had two wives the one called Adah the other Zillah by his first Wife Adah he begat Jabell and his brother Juball & of Zillah she bare Tuball-Caine and his Sister who was called Naamah.   And these Foure children found the begining of all these Crafts and Sciences in the world For the Eldest son Jabell found the craft of Geometrie and he fed flocks of Sheep and Lambs in the Field and first wrought houses of stone and he and his brother **Juball** Found the Craft of MUSIQUE song of mouth HARPP ORGAN and all other Instruments the Third brother **Tuball-Caine** found the smith craft ot Gold sillver Iron Copper and Steell and the daughter found the craft of weaveing. And these Children knew well that **God** would take vengance for sinn either by Fire or Water wherefore they wrote these **Sciences** they had Founded in two Pillers of stone that they might be found afterwards the one stone was called Carystius for that would not burn in the Fire And the other was called Latherne and that would not be drownded with Water. Our **Entent** is to tell you how and in what maner these stones were found that these **Sciences** was written on. the **Herminerius** that was Cubb his son the which Cubb was Semmett son the which was Noah's son this same **Herminerius** was afterwards called **Armes** the Father of the Wisemen he found one of the two Pillers ot stone and found the **Sciences** written therein and he taught itt to others, and at the makeing of the Tower of **Babilon** was **Masons** first there made much of and when the **King** of BABILON called **Membroth** who was a **Mason** himselfe and loved well the rest as is said with the Master of Stories And when the City of Neneve or the City of the East port should have been made **Nembroth** the **King** of **Babilon** sent thither Sixty **Masons** of his Reigon to the **King** of NINIVE his Cuzzon and when he sent them forth he gave them a Charge in this manner

First that they should be true to their **King** Lord or Master they served And that they should ordaine the most wise and cunning man to be Master of the **King** or Lords worke that was amongst them and neither for Love riches or faviour to sett another that had litle cunning to be Master of that worke whereby the Lord should be ill served and the **Science** ill Dishamed.

Secondly, that they should call the Governour of the said worke Master all the time they wrought with him and other many more charges were too long to cyte and for the keeping all those charges he made them sweare a great Oath which men used at that time and ordained for them reasonable pay that they might live with honesty and allso he gave them in charge They should Assemble together every yeare once to see how they might worke best to serve the **King** or Lord for their profitt and their own worshipp.

Thirdly that they should correct within themselves those that had trespassed against the **Science** and thus was this Noble Craft first grounded there. And the worthy Mr. **Euclides** gave it the name of **Geomitrie** and how it was called throughout all the world **Masonrie.** **Long** after when the Children of Isreall were come into the Land of Berhest which is now called the Country of Jerusalem where KING **David** begun the **Temp.e** which is now called TEMPLM DEI and is now named with us the **Temple** of **Jerusalem** and the same **King David** loved **Masons** then right well and gave them good pay And he gave the Charges and manners that he learned in **Egypt** which were given by the worthy DOCTER **Euclides** and other more Charges that you shall hear afterwards and after the decease of **King David** then Raigned **Solomon David's** son and he performed out the **Temple** that his Father had begunn and he sent after **Masons** into diverse Lands and into diverse Countries and he gathered them together so that he had 24000 workers of stone and were all named **Masons** and he choosed out of them 3000 and were ordained to be Masts. Rulers and Governours of his worke and there was a **King** of an other Reigon which men called **Jram** and he loved well KING **Solomon** and gave him Timber to his worke and he had a son called...... that was Master of **Geomitrie** and was cheife Master of all his **Masons** that belonged to the TEMPLE both for Graveing Carveing and all other **Masonrie.**

L

This is witnessed in the **Bible** (in Libro Regium tertio & quarto) and this same **Solomon** confirmed both the Charges and the maners which his Father had given and thus was the worthy **Science** of **Masonrie** confirmed in that Countrie of **Jerusalem** and many other Kingdoms and Reigions—Men walked into diverse countries some because of Learning to learn more cunning and some to teach them that had but little cunning.   And so it befell that there was a man called **Namus Greecinus** who had been at the makeing of **Solomon's Temple** and he came to France and there he taught the men of that Land the **Science** of **Masonrie** and there was one of the **Royall Line** of France called **Carolus Marsell** a man that loved well the said Craft and tooke upon him the Rules and maners and after that **By the Grace of God** was elected to be **King** of **France** and when he was in his Esstate he helped to make those **Masons** that were non and gave them charges and maners as he had learned of other **Masons** and set them on worke and gave them good pay and confirmed them a Charter from year to yeare to hould their **Assemblie** where they would and cherished them right well And thus came this noble Craft into **France.**

England in that season stood void as Foraigne charge of **Masons** untill **St. Albons** time for in his day the **King** of **England** and that was as a .... that did wall the Town about which is now called **St. Albons** and **St. Albons** was a worthy KNIGHT and STEWARD to the **King** of his houshold and head Gouernour of his Realme and allso of the makeing of the walls of the said Town and he loved well **Masons** and cherished them much and made their pay right good for he gave them iijs. vid. a weeke and iijd. a day for the bearers of Burthens —before that time in all the Land a **Mason** tooke but one penny on the day and his meat till **Albon** mended itt.   And he gott them a Charter from the **King** and his Counsell for to hold a General Counsell and gave itt to name **Assemblie** thereat he was himselfe and did help to make **Masons** and gave them Charges as you shall heare afterwards.   Soon after the death of **St. Albons** there came diverse Warrs into **England** out of diverse Nations so that the good Rule of **Masons** was quite Disheired and put down untill the time of **King Aldiston** in his time there was a worthy **King** in **England** that brought this Land into good rest and he builded many great works and Buildings therefore he loved well **Masons** for he had a son called **Edwine** the which loved **Masons** much more than his Father did and he was so much practiz'd in **Geomitrie** that he delighted much to come and talke with **Masons** and to learn of them the Craft and after for the love he had to **Masons** and to the Craft he was made **Mason** at WINSOUER and he got of the **King** his Father a Charter and Commision once every yeare to assemble within the Realm where they would within **England** and to correct within themselves Faults and Trespasses that were done as touching the Craft and he held them an **Assemblie** at **Yorke** and there he made **Masons** and gave them Charges and taught them the maners and commands the same to be kept ever afterwards And tooke them a Charter and Commision to keepe theire **Assemblie** and ordained that it should be renewed from KING to **King** and when the **Assemblie** were gathered together he made a **Cry** that all OLD **Masons** or young that had any writeings or understandings of the Charges and maners that were made before their Lands wheresoever the were made **Masons** that they shd shew them forth They were found some in **French** some in **Greeke** and some in **Hebrew** some in **English** and some in other **Languages** and when they were read and overseen well the Intent of them all was understood to be all one.

And then he caused a Booke to be made thereof how this worthy Craft of **Masonrie** was first Found and he himselfe commanded and allso then caused that itt should be read at any time when it should happen any 𝕸𝖆𝖘𝖔𝖓 or 𝕸𝖆𝖘𝖔𝖓𝖘 to be made to give him or them theire Charges and from that time untill this day manners of 𝕸𝖆𝖘𝖔𝖓𝖘 hath been kept in this maner and forme as well as men might govern itt. And furthermore at diverse 𝕬𝖘𝖘𝖊𝖒𝖇𝖑𝖎𝖊𝖘 have been put and ordained diverse Cratches by the best advice of 𝕸𝖆𝖌ᵗˢ and 𝕱𝖊𝖑𝖑𝖔𝖜𝖘.

Tun unus ex semioribus tenta Librum et illi ponent manum suam super Librum.

𝕰𝖛𝖊𝖗𝖞 man that is a 𝕸𝖆𝖘𝖔𝖓 take good heed to these Charges (wee pray) that if any man find himselfe guilty of any of these Charges that he may amend himselfe or principally for dread of 𝕲𝖔𝖉 you that be charged to take good heed that yee keepe all these Charges well for it is a great perill for a man to foreswear himselfe upon a Booke.

𝕿𝖍𝖊 𝕱𝖎𝖗𝖘𝖙 𝕮𝖍𝖆𝖗𝖌𝖊 𝖎𝖘 that yee shall be true men to 𝕲𝖔𝖉 and the holy Church and to use no error or Herisie by your understanding and by wise men's teaching allso

𝕾𝖊𝖈𝖔𝖓𝖉𝖑𝖞 that yee shall be true Leige men to the 𝕶𝖎𝖓𝖌 of 𝕰𝖓𝖌𝖑𝖆𝖓𝖉 without Treason or any Falshood and that ye know no Treason or Trechery but yee shall give knowledge thereof to the 𝕶𝖎𝖓𝖌 or to his Counsell allso yee shall be true one to another (that is to say) every 𝕸𝖆𝖘𝖔𝖓 of the Craft that is 𝕸𝖆𝖘𝖔𝖓 allowed yee shall doe to him as yee would be done unto your selfe.

𝕿𝖍𝖎𝖗𝖉𝖑𝖞 and yee shall keepe truely all the Counsell that ought to be kept in the way of 𝕸𝖆𝖘𝖔𝖓𝖍𝖔𝖔𝖉 and all the Counsell of the 𝕷𝖔𝖉𝖌𝖊 or of the Chamber allso that yee be no Theife nor Theives to your knowledge free that yee shall be true to the 𝕶𝖎𝖓𝖌 Lord or Master that yee serve and truely to see and worke for his advantage.

𝕱𝖔𝖚𝖗𝖙𝖍𝖑𝖞 yee shall call all 𝕸𝖆𝖘𝖔𝖓𝖘 your Fellowes or your Bretheren and no other names.

𝕱𝖎𝖋𝖙𝖍𝖑𝖞 yee shall not take your Fellows Wife in villany nor deflower his daughter or servant nor put him to disworshipp.

𝕾𝖎𝖝𝖙𝖍𝖑𝖞 yee shall truely pay for your meat or drinke wheresoever yee goe to Table or board allso yee shall doe no villany there whereby the Craft or 𝕾𝖈𝖎𝖊𝖓𝖈𝖊 may be Slandered.

𝕿𝖍𝖊𝖘𝖊 be the Charges Generall to every true 𝕸𝖆𝖘𝖔𝖓 both Masters & Fellowes.

𝕹𝖔𝖜 𝖜𝖎𝖑𝖑 𝕵 𝕽𝖊𝖍𝖊𝖆𝖗𝖘𝖊 𝖔𝖙𝖍𝖊𝖗 𝕮𝖍𝖆𝖗𝖌𝖊𝖘 𝖘𝖎𝖓𝖌𝖑𝖊 𝖋𝖔𝖗 𝕸𝖆𝖘𝖔𝖓𝖘 𝖆𝖑𝖑𝖔𝖜𝖊𝖉 𝖔𝖗 𝖆𝖈𝖈𝖊𝖕𝖙𝖊𝖉.

𝕱𝖎𝖗𝖘𝖙 that no 𝕸𝖆𝖘𝖔𝖓 take on him no Lords worke nor other mans unless he know himselte well able to perform the worke so that the Craft have no Slander.

𝕾𝖊𝖈𝖔𝖓𝖉𝖑𝖞 allso that no Master take worke but that he take reasonable pay for itt So that the Lord may be truely served and the Master to live honestly and to pay his Fellows truely and that no Master or Fellow supplant others of theire worke (that is to say) that if he hath taken 𝕬 worke or else stand Master of any worke that he shall not put him out unless he be unable of cunning to make an end of his worke And no Master nor Fellow shall take no Apprintice for less then seaven yeares and that the Apprintice be free-born and of Limbs whole as a man ought to be and no Bastard and that no Master or Fellow take no allowance to be made 𝕸𝖆𝖘𝖔𝖓 without the Assent of his Fellows at the least six or seaven.

· 𝕿𝖍𝖎𝖗𝖉𝖑𝖞 that he that be made be able in all degrees that is free-born of a good kindred true and no Bondsman and that he have his right Limbes as a man ought to have.

Fourthly that a Master take no Apprintice without he have occupation to occupie two or three fellows at the least.

Fifthly that no Master nor Fellow put away any Lords worke to task that ought to be Journey worke.

Sixthly that every Master give pay to his Fellows and servants as they may deserve soe that he be not defamed with false workeing And that none slander another behind his backe to make him loose his good name.

Seaventhly that no Fellow in the house or abroad answear another ungodly or reproveably without a cause.

Eightly that every MASTER Mason doe reverence his Elder and that a Mason be no common plaier at the Cards Dice or hazzard nor at other unlawfull plaies through the which the Science and Craft may be dishonored or slandered.

Ninthly that no Fellow goe into the Town by night exept he have a Fellow with him who may beare him record that he was in an honest place.

Centhly that every Master and Fellow shall come to the Assemblie if itt be within Fifty Miles of him if he have any warning and if he have trespased against the Craft to abide the award of Masters and Fellows.

Eleventhly that every Master Mason and Fellow that hath trespassed against the Craft shall stand to the correction of other Masters and Fellows to make him accord and if they cannot accord to go to the Common Law.

Twelvethly that a Master or Fellow make not a mould stone Square nor Rule to no Lowen nor set no Lowen worke within their Lodge nor without to mould stone.

Thirteenthly that every Mason receve and cherish strange Fellowes when they come over the Countrie and set them on worke if they will worke as the manner is (that is to say) if the Mason have any mould Stone in his place he shall give him a mould stone and sett him on worke and if he have none the Mason shall refresh him with money unto the next Lodge.

Fourteenthly that every Mason shall truely serve his Master for his pay.

Fifteenthly that every Master shall truely make an end of his worke Taske or Journey whether soe it be.

These be all the Charges and Covenants that ought to be Read at the makeing of a Free Mason or Free Masons THE ALMIGHTY God OF Jacob who ever have you and me in his keepeing bless us now and ever Amen

---

William Bray Free-man of London and Free-mason.

Written by **Robert Padgett** Clearke to the WORSHIPPFULL Society of the FREE Masons of the CITY of LONDON in the second yeare of the RAIGNE of our most GRACIOUS SOVERAIGN LORD King James the SECOND of ENGLAND &c. Annoq Domini 1686.

Certified to be a true transcript of the Original Scroll by
     E. JACKSON BARRON, F.S.A., P.M. & Sec. "Lodge of Antiquity."

London, 6th December, 1871.

"ALNWICK MS." (R)

(A.D. 1701.)

𝕿𝖍𝖊 𝕸𝖆𝖘𝖔𝖓𝖘' 𝕮𝖔𝖓𝖘𝖙𝖎𝖙𝖚𝖙𝖎𝖔𝖓𝖘.

𝔇𝔯𝔞𝔴 near unto me, ye unlearned, and dwell in the house of learning.—*Ecclesiasticus*, Cap. li. ver. 23.

In the hand of the Craftsmen shall the word be commended.—*Ecclesiasticus,* Cap. ix. ver. 17.

𝕿𝖍𝖊 might of the Father of Heaven with the Wisdom of his Glorious Son, through the Grace and Goodness of the Holy Ghost, Three Persons in one Godhead, be with us att our beginning ; and Give us Grace soe to governe us here in oᵉ Liveing, Thatt we may come to his Bliss thatt never shall have ending. Amen.

Good Brethren and Fellowes, oᵉ Purpose is to tell you how and in whatt manner this craft of masonry was Begun and afterwards how it was Founded by Worthy Emperours and Princes and many other Worppᶫ men, and alsoe to them that be here, we will declare them. The Charge thatt doth belong to Every true Mason is to keep in good Faith, and if you take good head theretoe it is well worthy to be kept, for a worthy Craft and a Curious Science ; For there is Seaven Liberall Sciences of the which itt is one of them, and the names of the Seven Sciences be these—The First is Grammᵉ and thatt teacheth a man to speak Truely ; and to write Truely : The Second is Rhetoricke and thatt teacheth a man to speak fair and in subtil Terms. The Third is Logick thatt teacheth to Discern Trueth from falshood. The Fourth is Arithmaticke thatt teacheth to Reckon and number all manner of numbᵉˢ. The Fifth is called Geometry and it teacheth a man to mett and measure the Earth, and other things ; of which Science is Masonry. The Sixth is Musick that teacheth the Craft of Songs, Organs and Harpe and Trumpett. The Seaventh is called Astronomy thatt teacheth a man to know the course of the Sunne moon and Starrs ; These be the seaven Liberall Sciences which be all founded by that one science that is called Geometrie; For Geometrie teacheth a man mett and measure, Ponderation, and Weight of all manners of things on Earth, and there is noe man thatt worketh any craft but he worketh by some mett or measure, and noe man buyeth or selleth butt by some measure or weight, and all this Geometrie ; And Craftsmen and Marchᵗᵗˢ finde noe other of the seaven sciences, and Especially Plowmen, and Tillers of all manner of Graine, both corne, seeds, Vines, Plants, Setters of all other fruite, For neither Grammᵉ nor Astronomy, nor none of all these can finde a man one measure or mett, without Geometrie, Wherfor I think the Science of Geometrie is to be accounted above any of the Seaven Sciences.

Cap. 4th
Ver. 19th
How this worthy Science was first begunne, I shall tell. Before Noah's Flood, there was a man called Lameck as it is written in the 4 Chap. of Gen. : and this Lameck had two Wives. The one was called Adah, and the other Zillah ; By the first wife Adah he gott two Sons, the one

M

Ver. 20th
Ver. 21st
called
Tuball Cain
and Naamah

called Jaball, and the other Juball, and by the other wife Zillah he got a Son and Daughter, and the four children found the beginning of all Crafts in the world.   This Jaball was the elder Son, and he found the Craft of Geometrie, and he parted flocks, as of Sheep and Lambs in the fields, and first wrought Houses of Stone and Tree, as it is noted in the Chape aforesaid, and his Brother Juball found the crafte of Musick, of Songs, Organs and Harp.

Tuball Cain

The Third Brother found out Smith's craft to work Iron and steel, and their sister, Naamah found out the art of Weaving ; These children did know thatt God would take Vengeance for Sinne, Either by fire or water, wherefor they wrote these Sciences which they had found in Two Pillars of stone, thatt they might be found after the Flood.

The one stone was called Marbell—cannott burn with Fire, and the other was called Laturus, thatt cannott drown in the Water :

Our intent is to tell you truely, and in whatt manner these stones were found that the science was written on.

Gens 10th,
Ver. 8th.
alias Nimrod.

The Great Hermemes thatt was Son unto Cush, which was Son unto Shem, which was Son unto Noah : This same Hermemes was afterwards called Hermes the Father of Wisdom, he found one of the Two Pillars of Stones, and found the Science written thereupon, and he taught to other men ; And att the makeing of the Tower of Babylon, there was the Craft off Masonry first found, and made much of : And the King of Babylon who was called Nimbroth was a Mason himselfe and loved well the craft, and is soe reported of by Mastes of the Stories : And when the Citty of Ninevy and other Citties of the East should be Built Nimbroth the King of Babylon sent thither Sixty Masons att the desire of the King of Ninevey his cosen, and when they went forth he gave them a Charge on this manne (biz) :

Nimbroth's
Charge.

Thatt they should serve the Lord truely for his payment, and thatt they should be true one to another, and that they should Live truely together soe he might have Worship for sending them to him, and other charges he gave ym.   Moreover when Abraham and Sarah his wife went intoe Egypt, and there taught the seaven Liberall Sciences to the Egyptians, and he had a worthy Schole called Euclide, and he learned right well, and was Maste of all the Seaven Liberall Sciences.   And it befell in his days thatt the Lords and State of the Realm had soe many Sons, thatt they had begotten, some by their Wives, and some by other Ladyes of thatt Realme ; For that Land is whole layd and a replenished Generation, and they had nott Liveing competent for their children, wherefor they made much sorrow.   And the King of thatt Land Assembled a great Councill at a Parliamt to know they might mentain their children, and they could finde noe good way, soe they caused a cry to be made throughout the Realm, if there were any man thatt could inform him, thatt he should come unto him, and he should be well rewarded for his Travell, and should hold himselfe well pleased.

After this cry was made, came this worthy Clark Euclide and said to the King and all his Greatt Lords—If you will give me yoo children to govern and Teach them honestly as Gentlemen should be taught under condition thatt you will grant them and me a Commission thatt I may have Power to Rule them honestly, as thatt Science ought to be ruled, and the King with his Councill granted them anon and sealed them that Commission, and the worthy Docte took to him the Lord's sons and taught them the Science of Geometrie in practice for to work in stones all manne of work thatt belonged to building of Castles, all manne of Courts, Temples and Churches with all other Buildings, and he gave them a Charge in this manne.

Euclydes Charge in Egypt. First that they should be true unto the King—and to the Lord they served, and thatt they should live well together, and be true one to another, and thatt they should call one another Fellow, and nott servant nor his knave, nor other foul names ; and thatt they should truely serve for their Payment to their Lord, thatt they serve ; and thatt they should ordain the wisest of them to be Maiste of the said Lord's work, and neither for Love great Lineage nor Liveing nor Riches to sett any other thatt had little cunning for to be Maister of the Lord's work, whereby the Lord should be ill served, and they ashamed ; and thatt they should call the Governe of the work Maste of the work while they wrought with him, and many other charges which were too long to tell.

And to all the Charges he made them swear thatt great Oath thatt men used att thatt time to swear, and ordered for them Reasonable paymt that they might live by work honestly ; and alsoe thatt they come and assemble themselves together, thatt they might have Councill in their Crafte, how they might worke best to serve their Lord for his proffit and worship, and thus was the craft of Geometrie grounded there ; and thatt they correct themselves if they had trespassed, and that worthy Maste Euclide gave it the name of Geometrie, and it is called Masonry throughout all the land ever since. Long after the children of Israell were come intoe the land of Bless ; and it is now amongst us called the country of Jerusalem. King David began the Temple of Jerusalem, which with them is called *Templum Domini*; And the same King David loved Masons very well and cherished them, and gave them good paymt : And he gave them the charge and mannes as he had it out of Egypt given by Euclide, and other charges thatt you shall hear afterwards.

1st Ks. C. 5. V. 15 16. And after the decease of King David, Solomon thatt was Son to David performed out the Temple thatt his father had begun, and sent after Masons of diverse Lands. and gathered them together,, soe thatt he had fourscore Thousand Workers of Stone. And they were named Masons, and three Thousand of them which were ordained to be Mastes and Governe of this work.

And there was a King of another Region that men called Hiram, and he loved well King Solomon, and gave him Timber for his work : and he had a son thatt was named Ajuon, and he was Maste of Geometrie, and he was chief Maste of all his Masons and Mastes of all his Graveing and Carving works, and of all other Manne of Masonry thatt belonged to the Temple, and this is Witnessed in the Bible in Libro Regum prio Cap 5th. And this same Solomon confirmed both charges and mannes which his Father had given to Masons, and after this manne was thatt worthy Craft of Masonry confirmed in the country of Jerusalem and many other Kingdoms. Glorious craftsmen walking about intoe diverse countrys, some because of Learning more craft, and some to teach their craft, and soe it befell that there was a curious mason named Naimus Græcus thatt had been att the makeing of Solomon's Temple, and came intoe France, and he taught the craft of masonry to the men of France. And soe there was one of the Royall Lyne of France that was called Charles Martiall, and was a man that loved well such a craft, and drew to him this Naimus Græcus abovesaid, and learned of him the craft and took upon him the charges, and afterwards by the Grace of God was elected King of France, And when he was in his stall he took to him many

Masons and made Masons there that were none, and set them on work, and gave them both charges and manners which he had learned of other Masons and confirmed them a Charter from year to year to hold their Assembly, and cherished them much, and thus came the craft into France.

England all this time stood void of any charge of Masonry, untill the time of Sᵗ Alban, and in his time, the King of England thatt was a Pagan and he walled a Town that is now called Sᵗ Albons, and in thatt Sᵗ Albons was a worthy Knight which was chief steward to the King and Governe of the Realm, and alsoe of making of the Town Walls and he loved Masons well, and cherished them, and he made their paymᵗ right good standing pay, as the Realm did require, for he gave them every week, Three shillings six pence, their double wages befor thatt time, throughout all the Land a Mason took butt a penny yᵉ day and meat untill the time that Sᵗ Albon amended it, and gave them a chartᵉ of the King and his Councill, and gave it the name of Assembly, and thereatt he was himselfe and made Masons and gave them a charge as you shall hear afterwards.

Right soon after the decease of Sᵗ Albon there came great Warrs intoe England of Divers nations soe thatt good rule of Masonry was destroyed, unto the time of King Athelstone thatt was a worthy King in England, who brought the Land intoe great rest and peace, and builded many great works of Abbeys, Castles, and many other buildings, and he loved Masons well. And he had a Sonn that was named Edwine; and he loved Masons more then his Fathe did, for he was full of Practice in Geometrie wherefor he drew him to common Masons to learn of them their Craft and after for the love he had to Masons and to the Craft he was made Mason himself, and he gott of his Father the King a Chartᵉ and Commission to hold every year an Assembly wherever he would within the Realm, and to correct within themselves faultes and Trespasses thatt were done within the Craft, And he held an Assembly att 𝔜orꬮ, and there he made Masons, and gave them charges and taught them the manne of Masons, and commanded that Rule to be holden for ever hereafter: and to them he gave the Chartᵉ and commission to keep and make ordinances thatt should be observed from King to King when this Assembly was gathered togethe he made a cry that all Masons both young and old thatt had any knowledge or understanding of the charges thatt were made in this Land, or in any other Land thatt they should shew them forth ; and there was found some in Greek some in English, some in French, and some in othe Languages ; and the Intent thereof was found and commanded thatt it should be read and told when any Mason was made, and to give him his Charge, and from that Day untill this present time Masons have been kept in thatt form and order ; as well as men might govern it. And furthermore at diverse Assemblyes there hath been putt and added certaine charges more and more by the best of advice from Maste and Fellows.

Then shall one of the most ancient of them all hold a Book that he or they may lay his or their hand or hands upon the said Book, and these precepts following ought then to be Read.

Every man thatt is a Mason take heed right well of this charge. If you find yoᵉself guilty of any of these, thatt you amend you again, and especially yee thatt are to be charged : Take heed thatt you may keep this charge for it is a great Perill for a man to forswear himself on a Book.

Edwine's Charge. The First charge is Thatt you shall be a True man to God and his holy Church and thatt you use noe heresy nor error to your understanding, or to desert discreet or wise men's Teaching, Alsoe you shall be a true Liege man to the King without Treason or falshood, and thatt you shall know noe Treason, but thatt you mend it and you may, or else warne the King or his Councill thereof : Alsoe you shall be true one to another (that is to say) to every Mast⁰ and Fellow of the Craft of Masonry thatt be Masons allowed. Thatt you would do to them, as you would they should doe to you. Alsoe thatt every Mason keep true Councill of Lodge of Chamb⁰, and all other Councill, that ought to be kept by way of Masonry :

Also that noe man shall be Thief, nor Thief's see soe far as you shall know. Alsoe thatt you shall be true to yo⁰ Lord and Mast⁰ thatt you serve, and truely to see his Profitt and Advantage. Alsoe that you shall call Masons yo⁰ Fellows and Brethren ; and by noe other Foul Name, nor you shall nott take yo⁰ Fellows wife in Villany' or desire ungodly his daughte or his servant to his Villany, Alsoe you shall pay truely for yo⁰ Table and meat and drinke where you goe to Board, and alsoe thatt you doe noe Villany in thatt house whereby the craft should be slandered, These be the charges in Generall that a Mason should hold both Mast⁰⁰ and Fellows.

Rehearse I will now other charges singular for Masters and Fellows. First that noe Mast⁰ shall take any work of a Lord, or any other work butt thatt he know himself able and cunning to performe the same, soe thatt the craft have noe disworship, but thatt the Lord may be well and truely served ; Alsoe that noe Mast⁰ take any work, but that he take it reasonably, soe thatt the Lord may be truely served with his own goods, and the Mast⁰ to live honestly, and pay his Fellows truely their pay as the mann⁰ of the craft doth require ; Alsoe thatt noe Mast⁰ or Fellows subplant others of these works (thatt is to say) if he hath taken a worke or stand Mast⁰ of a Lord's work ; you shall nott putt him out, if he be able and cunning of craft to end the work ; Alsoe thatt noe Mast⁰ or Fellows take noe Apprentice to be allowed his Apprentice butt for seaven yeares, And thatt Apprentice be able of his Birth and Limbs as he ought to be. Alsoe that noe Mast⁰ or Fellows take noe allowance to be made without the assent of his Fellows, and thatt att the least Five or Six. And that he thatt shall be made Mason be able over all Sciences—(thatt is to say) that he be free born, and of good Kindred, and noe Bondman, and thatt he have his right Limbs, as he ought to have : Alsoe thatt noe Mast⁰ putt noe Lord's work to task, thatt was wont to goe to Journey.

Alsoe thatt every Mast⁰ shall give to his Fellows, butt as he may deserve, soe thatt he be nott deceived by false worke. Alsoe thatt noe Fellow slander one falsly behinde his back to make him loose his good Name or his worldly goods.

Alsoe that noe Fellow wᵗʰ in the Lodge nor without misanswer another neither ungodly or irreverently without reasonable cause. Alsoe thatt mason preferr his Elder and put him to worshipp. Alsoe thatt noe Mason should play att Hazard or any othe⁰ unlawfull game whereby they may be slandered : Alsoe that noe mason be a common Rebell in leachery to make the craft to be slandered and thatt noe Fellow goe intoe the Town in the Night time, where is a Lodge of Fellows, without a Fellow thatt may bear him witnesse thatt he was in an honest place : Alsoe thatt every mason and Fellow come to the Assembly if it be within Fifty miles about him ; if he have reasonable warning and stand there att the award of Mast⁰ and Fellows : Also thatt every Mast⁰ and Fellow if they have Trespassed one to another shall stand the award of Mast⁰ and Fellows to make them accord if they may ; and if they may not accord, then to goe to Common Law ; Alsoe thatt noe mason make moulds, Square or Rule to any Rough Layers, Alsoe thatt noe Mason sett any Layer within a Lodge or without to Hew or mould stones with noe mould of his own makeing—Alsoe thatt every mason shall cherish and receive strange Fellows, when they come over the countrey and sett them on work as the manne is (thatt is to say) if they have mould stones in place, he shall sett him a fortnight att the least on work, and give him his hyre : And if there be noe Stones ʻor him to work, he shall refresh him with money, to bring him to the next Lodge. And alsoe you and every mason shall serve truely the workers, and truely make an end of your work, be it Task or Journey; if you have your pay, as you ought to have.

𝕿𝖍𝖊𝖘𝖊 𝕮𝖍𝖆𝖗𝖌𝖊𝖘 thatt we have reckoned, and all other thatt belongeth toe Masonry you shall truely keep and well observe, so helpe you God and Holy-doome; and this Book, to the uttermost of your Power.

FINIS.

Gra : Loquitz : Lo : vera docet : Rhe : verba solorat : Mu : canit. Ar : Numeratt: Ge: Ponderat

Ast : capit Astra.

Transcribed from the original Scroll by W. J. Hughan.

"PAPWORTH'S MS." (T)

(*About A.D. 1714.*)

IN GOD IS ALL OUR TRUST

𝕿𝖍𝖊 𝖒𝖎𝖌𝖍𝖙 of the Father of Heaven with the wisdom of his blessed Son through the grace of God & goodness of the Holy Ghost yt be three persons in one Godhead be with us at our beginning & give grace so to govern us here in this life living, that we may come to his Bliss that never shall have ending. Amen.

Good Brethren & Fellows Our purpose is to tell you how & in what manner this worthy Craft of Masonry was begun & afterwards how it was founded by worthy Kings & Princes & many other worshipfull men & also to them that that be here we will declare the Charges that belong to every true Mason to keep for in good truth if yt you take good heed it is well worthy to be kept well for a worthy Craft & curious Science. For there are Seven liberal Sciences of the which Seven it is one of them, & the names of the Seven be these. The first Gramar, and that teacheth a man to Speak truely & write truely, and the second is Rhetorick, & that teacheth a man to speak fair & in sublime terms, & ye third is Logick & that teacheth a man to discerne truth from falshood, and the fourth is Arithmetick and that teacheth a man to reckon & account all manner of Numbers, And the fifth is Geometry and that teacheth met & measure of either & so all other things, of the wch Science is annexed Masonry, And the Sixth Science is called Musick and yt teacheth a man Song and voice of tongue & Organ Harp & Trumpet And the Seventh Science is called Astronomy and that teacheth a man to know the course of the Sun of the Moon & of the Starrs. These be the Seven liberal Sciences, the which seven be all founded by one that is Geometry and this may a man prove that the Science of the work is founded by Geometry for Geometry teacheth met & measure ponderation & weight of all manner of things on earth ; for their is no man that worketh any Craft but he worketh by some met or measure nor no man that bieth & selleth, but he byeth & getteth by some met or measure or byeth by some weight, and all this is Geometry, and these Merchants and all Crafts & all other of these Seven Sciences & especialy the Plowman & Tillers of all manner of Grain & seeds, vine flowers, & setters of other fruit. For in Gramar nor Rhetorick nor Astronomy nor in any other of all the Seven liberal Sciences can no man finde met or measure without Geometry wherefore we think that this Science of Geometry is most worthy & foundeth to all others.

How that these worthy Sciences was first begun I shall you tell. Before Noahs Flood there was a man called Lamech as it is written in the Bible in ye 4 Chapter of Genesis & this Lamech had 2 wives, the name of the one was Adah & the other was Zillah, by this wife Adah he got 2 Sonns and the one he named Jabel & the other Tubal, and by the other wife Zillah he begat a Son and a Daughter, and these 4 Children founded the beginning of all the Crafts in the World, & his eldest Son Jabel founded the Craft of Geometry, he had flocks of Sheep & lands in the fields, & first wrought in hewing of Stone and tree as it is noted in the Chapter above said, and his brother Jubal founded yͤ Craft of Musick song and tongue Harp & Organ, & the third brother Tubal Cain founded the Craft called Smith Craft of Gold silver Copper, Iron & brass & steel & yͤ Daughter found the Craft of Weaving.

And these Children knew well yᵗ God would take vengeance for Sin either by fire or water wherefore they did write the Sciences they had found in two Pillars of Stone that they might be found after Noah's flood, and the one Stone was Marble for it would not burn with fire, and the other Stone was called Latirnes & yᵗ would not drown with water.   Our intent is to tell you how these Stones was found in which the Sciences was written.

The great Hermes was Cub his Son, yͤ wᶜʰ Cub was him that was Noah's Son. These Harmarines was afterwards called Hermes the Father of wise men.   He found one of the 2 Pillars of Stone and he found the Sciences written therein and he taught it to other men.   And at the making of the Tower of of Babilon there was Masonry made much of, & the hight Nimrod was a Mason himself & loved well the Craft as it is said with Masters of Histories, And when the city of Ninive & other Cities of the East should be made, Nimrod of Babel sent thither 60 Masons at the Rogation of the King of Ninive his Cosin & when he sent them forth he gave them a Charge in this manner that they should be true to each other that they should love truely together & yᵗ they should serve their Lord for their pay so their Master might have worship & all that belong to him & other more Charges he gave them, and this was the first time that ever Mason had any Charge of his Craft.

Moreover when Abraham and Sarah his wife went into Egypt & there he taught the 7 Sciences to the Egyptians, and he had a worthy Schollar the hight Euclyd & he learned right well & was a Master of all the 7 liberal Sciences, and in his days it befell that yͤ lords of yͤ States of yͤ Realm had many Sons yt they had gotten some by their wifes & some by their Ladyes of that Realm, for yᵗ land is a hot land & plenteous in generation & they had not a competent living to finde their Children & wherefore they had much care, & then the King of that land made a great Counsel & a Parliament to wit how they might find their Children honestly as Gentleman, & they could find no manner of good way, & then they did Cry through all the Realm that if there were any man that could informe them that he should come to them & he should be well rewarded for his travel that he should hold.   After this Cry was made then came this worthy Clark Euclyd & he said to the King & to all the great Lords if you will take me to your Children to govern & to teach them one of the Seven Sciences wherewith they may live honestly as Gentlemen should under condition that he will grant me & them a Comission that I may have power to Rule them after the manner that the Science ought to be ruled & the King & all his Counsel granted him & sealed their Comission and then this worthy Doctor took to him these Lords & taught the Science of Geometry in practice to worke in Stones all manner of worthy work that belongeth to buildings Churches & Temples Castles & Towers Mannors & all other manner of Buildings.   And he gave them a Charge in this manner.

The first was that they should be true to their King & to the Lord that they owe & yᵗ they should love well together & to be true each one to another & that they should call each one his fellow or else his brother and not his Servant or Knave, or any foul name, & that they should truely deserve their pay of their Lord or the Master yᵗ they serve, & they should ordain the wisest of them to be Master of the work & neither for love nor great Linage, riches nor favour to set another yᵗ hath little cunning for to be Master of the Lords work whereby the

Lord shall be evil served & they ashamed. And also that they should call ye Governor of the Work Master in the time that they work with him, and other many more Charges he made that it is too long to tell, and to all the Charges he made them to swear a great Oath that men used at that time & also ordained for them reasonable pay or wages that they might live honestly, And also that they should come & assemble together every year once how they might work best to serve the Lord for his profit & to their own worship & to correct within themselves him that had trespassed against the Craft, & thus was the Craft grounded there, And that worthy Mr Euclyd gave it the name of Geometry and now it is called Masonry through out all the land. Sith long after when the Children of Israel did come into the land of the Behest that is now called amongst us the Country of Jerusalem David began the Temple of the Lord that is called Templum Domini which is called the Temple of Jerusalem & this King David loved well Masons & cherished them much & gave them good pay & he gave them the Charge & the manner as he had learned in Egypt Euclid gave them, and Charges more yt you shall hear afterwards, And after the decease of King David Solomon that was King Davids Son performed out the Temple yt his Father had begun and he sent after Masons into divers Countries of divers lands & gat them together so that he had 80 thousand workers of Stone & were all called Masons & he choosed out three thousand that were ordained to be Masters & Governors of his Works. And furthermore there was a King of another Region that men called Hiram & he loved well King Solomon and he gave him cunning men to work, & had a son that was called Benaim & he was a Master of Geometry & was Master of all his Masons and Carving and of all other manner of Works belonging to the Temple and this is witnessed in the Book of Kings called Libro Regum Cap. 30.

This Solomon gave Orders Charges & Manners that his Father had gotten of the Masons & thus was this worthy Craft Confirmed in the Country of Jerusalem, & in many other Kingdoms curious Craftsmen were sent full wide into divers Countries some because of learning more Craft & Cunning, & some to teach those that have little Cunning & it befell that there was one cunning Mason that hight Nimus Graneus that had been at the making of Solomons Temple, & he came into France & there he taught the Science of Masonry to men of France. And there was one a Regalian of France that hight Charles of Merten & he was a man that loved well such Craft & Nimus Graneus that is above said & he learned of him the Craft & took upon him ye Charge & manner & afterwards was elected to be King of France & when he was in his estate he took Masons & did undertake to make men Masons that were none & gave them both the Charge & manner how to pay as he had learned of other Masons & confirmed them a Charter from year to year, & to hold their Assembly where they would & cherrished them much, & thus came the Craft into France. England all this time stood void for any charge of Masonry untill St. Albans time & in his time the King of England was a Pagan, about that yt is called St. Albans, & St. Alban was a worthy Knight and Steward of the King & of his Household & had Government of his Realm & also of making the Town walls & loved well Masons & cherrished them right much & he made their pay right good standing as the Realm did for he gave them 2 Shillings & Six pence a week & three pence for their nuncions and before yt time throughout all the land a Mason took but a penny a day untill St. Alban amended it & gave them a a Charge of the King & of his Counsell for to hold a general Assembly or Counsel & gave it the name of Assembly & thereat he was himselfe & helped to make Masons, and gave them the Art as you shall heare afterwards. Right soon after the decease of St. Alban there came divers warrs into England

N

out of divers Nations so that the good Rule of Masonry was destroyed untill the time of King Athelston that was a worthy King of England & brought this land into rest & builded many great Works as Abbies & Towers and all other manner of buildings, & loved well Masons, And he had a son y^t hight Edwin & he loved Masons much more then his father & was a great practiser in Geometry & he drew to Masons & loved much to talk and comune with them & to learn of them the Craft he was made a Mason & he gat of the King his Father a Charter & Comission to hold every year one Assembly wheresoever they would within the Realm of England and to correct within themselves defaults & the Trespasses that were done within the Craft, & he held himself an Assembly at 𝔜𝔬𝔯𝔨 & there he made Masons and gave them Charges & taught them ye Manner and comanded that rule to be kept ever after & took them the Charter & Comission to keep and made Ordinances y^t it should be renewed from King to King & when the Assembly was gathered together he made a Cry y^t all old Masons & young that had any writing or understanding of the Mannors & Charges that were made before in this Land or in any other that they should shew them forth & wheu it was proved there was tound some in French & some in Greek & some in other Languages & the intent of them was found all one, and he made a Book thereof how the Craft was founded And he himself bad and Comanded that it should be read or told y^t when any Mason should be made for to give his Charges and from that day to this time the Manner of Masons have been kept in that form as men might govern it Furthermore at divers Assemblies hath been put & ordained certain Charges by the best advice of Masters & Fellows.

Tunc unus ex senioribus tenet Librum ut illc illi ponant manus super Librum & tunc præcepta deberent legi.

Every Mason that is a Mason take right good heed to these Charges if any man find himself guilty in any of these Charges against God that he amend, & principally ye y^t that are to be charged take good that ye may keep these Charges right well for it is a great perril for a man to forswear himself upon a Book.

𝕋𝕙𝕖 𝔽𝕚𝕣𝕤𝕥 ℂ𝕙𝕒𝕣𝕘𝕖.

That he or thou shall be true man to God & and to the holy Church & y^t he use neither Error nor heresy to your understanding or discreet or wise mens teaching.

And also that he shall be true leige-man to the King of England without treason or treachery but that ye amend it privately if ye may, or else tell the King or his Counsel.

And also ye shall be true one to another y^t is to say to every Mason of the Craft of Masonry y^t be Masons allowed ye shall do to them as you would they should do to you.

And also that ye keep truely all the Counsel of the Lodg & of the Chamber & all other Counsel y^t ought to be kept by way of Mason-hood.

And also y^t no Mason be theivish or a Thief but as far forth as he may use honestly his wit or knowledge.

And also you shall be true to the Lord or to the Master you serve & truely see his profit and advantage.

And also you shall call Masons y^r Brethren or else y^r Fellows but no other foul name.

And also you shall not take in villany your Fellows wife nor desire ungodly his daughter nor his Servant nor put him to disworship.

And also y^t y^u pay truely for y^r meat & your drink where you go to board.

And also that you do no Villany in that place where you go to board whereby the Craft may be slandered.

These be the Charges in generall that belong to every true Mason to be kept both Masters & Fellows.

Rehearse in general other Charges for Masters & Fellows.

First that no Mason shall take upon him any Lords work or other mens work but that he knoweth himself able & sufficient of cunning to performe the same Lords work so that y$_e$ Craft have no slander nor disworship but that the Lord may be well served & truely.

And also that no Master take any work but that he take it reasonably so that the Lord may be truely served with his own good & the Master to live honestly & to pay his fellows truely as the manner is.

And also that no Master nor fellow shall supplant others of their work y$_t$ is to say yt he hath taken a work or else stand Master of the Lords work ye shall not put him to work unless he be able of cunning to perform or end the same work.

And also that no Master nor Fellow take no Prentis within the term of seven years & the Prentis be able of Birth free born & of limbs whole as a man ought to be.

And that no Master nor Fellow take no allowance to make any Mason without the assent and consent of his Fellows six or else seven at the least, & he that shall be made Mason be able in all manner of degrees that is to say free born & of good kindred & true & no bondman & also that he have his right limbs as a man ought to have.

And also that no Mason shall take any Prentis unless he have sufficient occupation for to occupy one or two or three fellows at the least.

And also that no Master nor Fellows put no Lords work to texen y^t was wont to go to Jornay.

And also that Every Master shall give pay to his Fellows but as he may deserve so y^t he may not be decoyed by false workmen.

And also y^t none shall slander another behind his back to loose his good name or else his worldly riches.

And also that no Fellow within the Lodge or or without misanswer another ungodly or ribaldry without a cause.

And also that every Mason shall reverence his elder and put him to worship.

And also y^t no Mason shal be no comon Player at hazard or at y$_e$ Dice nor no unlawful game whereby the Craft might be slandered.

And also y^t no fellow go into the Tavern on nights there that is a lodg of Fellows without he have a Fellow with him y^t he may bear witness that he was in honest play.

And also y^t every Mason & Fellow shall come to y^e Association if it be within 5 miles about him if he have any warning & if he have trespassed against the Craft shall stand there at ye award of Master & Fellows, & to make them accord if they may & if they may not accord then to go to ye common law.†

Certified by Mr. Wyatt Papworth to be a true copy, March, 1872.

† Remainder is lost.

"KRAUSE'S MS." (Z)

(Translation.)

The Constitution completed by the pious (Prince) Edwin begins:

The omnipotence of the eternal God, Father and Creator of the heavens and the earth, the wisdom of his divine Word, and the influence of his given Spirit, be with our beginning, and grant us grace so to govern ourselves in this life, that we may obtain His approval here, and everlasting life after death.

The good brethren desire ; first, to know how and in what manner the venerable art of architecture began ; but after that, how it has been preserved, and how it has flourished by the aid of kings and princes. Then they wish to know also, which of those laws, introduced by St. Alban, after the manner of the Romans, are still good and useful. As now the Romans and Greeks, already held the art of architecture to be worthy of faithful observance as a great art and remarkable science, so shall it be according to the wish of the pious king. But this is the beginning and progress of this art.

History of the Origin and Progress of Masonry beyond the confines of Britain.

When the first man had gone, with all his mental and physical advantages, out of the hand of God, he soon sinned against his Creator, and the consequence was, that as a punishment, he soon felt the effects of the weather, to protect himself from which, he was compelled to consider. But with the lofty intellect which he had received from God, and as God himself had taught him the art of writing, it could not be otherwise than that he should think of a dwelling place, and lay down rules in all the other necessary sciences which had been discovered, so that his posterity might be guided thereby. Hence, therefore, Cain built the first town, (and with this began to flourish the art of building regular houses in the East,) Cain's son Enoch, in particular, was a great architect and astronomer, he foresaw in the stars, that the world should be destroyed once by water, and again by fire, and made therefore two great pillars, one of stone and the other of clay, upon which he inscribed the fundamental rules of the art, so that the science of Adam and his posterity might not be lost. The art of working in iron had been already brought to perfection by Tubal Cain, the art of weaving by Naamah ; and by her brother Jabal the breeding of cattle, agriculture, and the setting up of tents, which people afterwards used in war.

All the posterity of Adam preserved these arts, until at last Noah planted the vine and received instruction from God, in the earliest laws of men from the creation of the world, and was taught to build a great floating house of wood, by which the art of ship-building was originated, which the people of Soria (Phœnicia,) were afterwards the first to use.

Two generations after Noah, his descendants, proud of their knowledge, built on the plain of Shinar, a great city and a high tower of lime, stones, and wood, in order that they might dwell together, under the laws which their ancestor Noah had made known, and that the names of Noah's descendants might be preserved for all time. This arrogance however did not please the Lord in heaven, the lover of humility, therefore he caused a confusion of languages among them before the tower was finished, and scattered them in many uninhabited lands, whither they brought with them their laws and arts, and then founded Kingdoms and Principalities, as the divine Scriptures often testify. Nimrod in particular, built a town of considerable size ; but Noah's son Shem remained in Ur in the land of the Chaldeans, and spread a knowledge of all the sciences and arts abroad, and taught also Peleg, Serug, Nahor, Terah, and Abraham ; the last of whom, knew all the sciences, and had knowledge, and continued to instruct the sons of free-men, whence, afterwards, the numerous learned priests and mathematicians, who have been known under the name of the Chaldean magi. Abraham continued to propagate the arts and sciences farther when he came to Egypt, and found there, in Hermes particularly, so apt a scholar, that the latter was at last termed the Trismegistus of the sciencies, for he was at once Priest and Naturalist in Egypt, and through him and a scholar of his, the Egyptians received the first good laws and all the sciences, in which Abraham had instructed him. Subsequently Euclid collected the principal sciences which he named Geometry, but the Greeks & Romans called them Architecture.

In consequence of the confusion of languages the knowledge of the arts and sciences could not be extended, until people had learnt to make comprehensible by signs what they could not understand from words. Hermes brought the custom of making himself understood by signs with him to Egypt, when he filled with inhabitants a valley by the Nile. Thence afterwards, this art came into all distant lands ; but only the signs which are given by the hands have remained in Architecture, for the signs of the figures are as yet known to but few.

In Egypt the overflowing of the Nile gave opportunity to exercise the arts of measuring and building bridges and dykes which Mizraim introduced. They used burnt bricks (*Steine,*) wood, and earth ; therefore all this became known to the heathen kings who were compelled to prepare stones, lime, and bricks, and to erect buildings therewith, by which means however, by God's will, they only became the more experienced artists, and became so celebrated, that their art spread as far as Persia. After this, Moses led this chosen people out of Egypt to Canaan, and caused their artists to build the most celebrated ark of the covenant of wood and iron, and wrought (*worked*) gold. He brought above all the art of Architecture to great perfection, because wisdom was in him. The old inhabitants it is true, already built with stone, and had certainly already houses and towns, and palaces, but the sacred architecture which had been used in the building of the ark sur-passed all others.

When Joshua had brought the ark to Shiloh, the priests served God around it, and tilled land, as it was tilled in Egypt, and as it still is, for the benefit of man-kind.

From this time the art of building with lime, stone, and wood, spread even further, and the people of Phœnicia in particular distinguished themselves therein, for they built the cities of Tyre and Sidon, which their kings afterwards caused their artists to beautify. Among these, King Hiram distinguished himself above all, and became therefore so celebrated, that the Israelitish king Solomon, when he proceeded to erect the sacred Temple to God, which his father had projected, begged him (Hiram), to send skilful artificers and workmen. For the Phœnicians excelled also in the sacred art of building, and had excellent architects, one of whom, Sanchiston, erected the temple of Dagon, an artistic, noble, and spacious sacred edifice, which held 3000 persons, although they offered sacrifices to false gods therein. And it was the same also in other lands.

Though spacious and excellent buildings were already formed every where, they all remained far behind the sacred Temple which the wise King Solomon caused to be erected in Jerusalem in honor of the true God, where he employed an uncommonly large number of workmen, as we find in the Holy Scriptures, and the King Hiram of Tyre added a number, among these assistants was King Hiram's most skilful architect, whose name was Hiram Abif, the son of a widow, and who afterwards made the most excellent fittings, and the most costly work, which are all described in the Holy Scriptures. The whole of these artificers were divided into certain classes, and thus at this great building was founded, for the first time, a worthy (venerabiles), Society of Architects (Societas Architectonica). Similar arrangements were afterwards made by the Greeks and Romans, and from the Romans, they afterwards came over the sea to us here, from Italy and Gaul. These divisions arose from the division of the artificers, according to the nature of their work, into Collegia or Lodges, each of which had a Master *(Magister fabricae)*, and several wardens, hence it followed that the directions of the Architect could be punctually carried out ; they had at the same time to care for the tools and materials, and the weekly payments, as well as the food and articles of clothing to give out. It was also necessary to constantly attract appentices, so that workmen should never be wanting. Thus arose a complete union among them all, and as the Master and Wardens received the directions from the Architect also, a union of all these lodges with each other resulted, and love and friendship bound them all together so strongly, that each one divided his superfluities with his necessitous brother, and thus they corrected not only the errors in their work, but those in themselves.

Probably under just such excellent arrangements, and by the aid of the numerous workmen, Solomon's admirable work, (which could contain 30,000 persons) was erected, to the astonishment of all the neighbouring nations, (from whom competent judges came to Jerusalem,) in seven years and six months, by Solomon the wisest of mankind, with all its splendid and complete internal arrangements, *(fittings.)* After it was finished, they kept a general feast, and the joy over the happy completion, was only dimmed by the death soon after, of the excellent Master Hiram Abif. They buried him before the Temple, and he was mourned for by all. Thus the extraordinary architecture, employed on this sacred edifice was spread abroad : and it was held in great repute by all nations. Many Architects and skilful workmen, who had helped to complete the edifice, availed themselves of this, and now wandered far around, in order to teach those who were less skilful ; in doing which, they made similar arrangements to those which they had learnt in Jerusalem. One of these, named Ninus with his companions, reached the Western coasts in a Phœnician ship, thus it happened that he was the first to introduce the Oriental Architecture on those coasts, whence it spread abroad into the countries of the West. The remainder stayed in Jerusalem, as King Solomon wanted their help, to erect his palaces, and other excellent edifices.

After Solomon's Temple had stood 430 years, it was destroyed by Nebuchadnezzar. He also led many building artificers prisoners to Bablyon, and erected very excellent buildings. These edifices, were, it is true, far from equalling the architecture which Solomon had used, but the remarkable art of architecture was, however, preserved in this manner, and continued, until the great Cyrus, afterwards let the Jews return again to Jerusalem and gave Zerubbabal orders to build up the Temple again upon the same spot. It is true, Cyrus died while the work was in progress, but it was continued under Darius ; after twenty years' labour it was completed, and the building feast held. This Temple, also, was such an excellent building, that even the Jews' enemies admired it, although it was not equal to the first Temple. Zerubbabel's Temple stood until the time of Antoninus and Octavius when it was pulled down by their governor Herod, who caused to be again built, upon the same spot, the third Temple, in Grecian style by Grecian Architects, and this also was very magnificent.

Many workmen laboured thereon nine years and six months, before they could celebrate the builders' feast.

At this time the knowledge of Architecture had been spread as far as the West, by the Phœnicians, who navigated the sea in all directions for trading purposes ; in Greece also it had attained great perfection, and we find many splendid large buildings throughout the whole of Greece, all of which had been first caused by Solomon's Temple, in consequence of the admiration it excited in all the neighbouring nations. The navigation in the West was prosecuted by the Romans, who thus came to Greece and the East.

Pythagoras, the Greek, in particular, promoted Architecture. He travelled into Egypt, and Syria, and to all parts where it flourished. He was admitted into lodges, and on his return gave instruction about them ; he then proceeded by sea to Greece and remained there, becoming very celebrated as a philosopher ; he founded also at Crotona the great School of Philosophy and Architecture, and he was the discoverer of many fundamental principles, which were afterwards applied to Geometry. He had many scholars, who, also, afterwards became philosophers, and were equally celebrated ; they, also, were the discoverers of many such fundamental principles, until the renowned Euclid of Tyre, brought all these principles together, and compiled a book, which it is necessary for all architects to understand. After the time of Euclid all the sciences were regularly taught, and were divided into Grammar, Rhetoric, Logic, Arithmetic, Geometry, Music, and Astronomy. All these seven arts an Architect must know; therewith, however, he must also know other sciences of the Romans, for which reason it is very difficult to be an architect. Still, Geometry will always remain the basis of Architecture, and it is sufficient that those who are not Architects, make themselves thoroughly acquainted with this (geometry) only.

As it was always difficult to become an Architect, the art was held in esteem by the Greeks, as it was only the free-born who were permitted to learn it, this being forbidden to the slaves. Thus it flourished, as in Athens, so in Carthage, in Etruria, and also upon the island of Syracuse, wherein the sage Archimides became so celebrated for his knowledge of geometry, and by his death in its pursuit.

The Romans drew their knowledge of the arts and sciences out of Etruria, Greece, Egypt, and Asia, and acquired a closer knowledge of them, through their wars. For this purpose, they carried celebrated and learned persons to their city ; and learned people from among themselves travelled into those places and returned again. Thus, Rome became, in course of time, the chief seat of learning, which reached its best period under the Emperor Augustus, who had done so much to promote it, and because under his government the Messiah was born ; Rome became afterwards the first capital in the West, in which the Gospel from the East took root.

The Emperor Augustus, had in his pay, the excellent Architect Vitruvius, of Rome, who was particularly celebrated, and by him very many excellent edifices were erected. Therefore we call the correct Architecture which Vitruvius again introduced, the Augustan. Vitruvius wrote a book on the subject of Architecture, this, and the book of Euclid must be understood by every Architect.

History of the Origin and Progress of Masonry in Britain.

But this art of building was brought by Italian and Gallic Architects to Britain. In the 43rd year after the birth of our Lord, the Emperor Claudius sent Architects from Rome to England, who had to build castles and towers, so that the Romans might be secure in Britain.   They taught others the Vitruvian art of Architecture, and so, during the life time of the Emperors Vespasian and Hadrian, were also built the walls against the northern nations ; but King Lud, *(Lucius,)* who was the first Christian King of Britain, built churches.   And as the Greeks and Romans had already instituted Lodges, this arrangement was also introduced in Britain, and thus it remained in some parts of England until the year of our Lord 300, when the Emperor Carausius caused a castle to be built in the town of Verulam, and a wall round the town, for which reason he caused yet more artificers to come from Rome.   He had a Roman Architect who was called Amfiabulus, and he became the teacher, *(Doctor,)* of St. Alban, whom the Emperor appointed to manage the erection of the buildings, because he was at the head of his household.   St. Alban, a worthy Roman knight, took to the art, because he had grown fond of it ; he loved the workmen, and gave them great support.   He made Constitutions and charges for the Masons, and taught them the customs ; every thing as Amfiabalus had taught him.   He procured for them also good pay, for he gave to the workmen two shillings per week, and three pence for their food, while formerly they had only had one penny and their food.   He also obtained a charter from the Emperor Carausius, according to which the workmen in the whole of Britain, were made into a Society by themselves, and were placed under the Architects, which had not been the case before, as each individual had taken work whereever he found it to do.   St. Alban belonged to this Society himself, helped to admit new workmen, and took care that they had always plenty of work ; and he was the first who did this in Britain.   His death must have been a great grief to the Society, for the Emperor, having learned that he had secretly become a Christian, he was, like John, executed as a Confessor of the Faith, and thus became the first martyr in Britain, as the former had been the first martyr among the Christians.

Persecution overcame them, and the art lay in the dust, until it was again raised by the Emperor Constantine and under his son (the Emperor Constantine) the Christian religion flourished, when some churches and large edifices were erected in the Roman style of Architecture.

Wars, however, again took place with the northern nations, (Picts and Scots,) and as these obtained the mastery, the Romans withdrew from the government of England ; the Britons were therefore compelled to call the Angles and Saxons to help them ; and then the art was again laid low, because these nations were heathens, and the war was continued.

At last, however, there was a return to peace, and the Bishop of Rome, caused the Angles and Saxons to be converted to the Christian faith, through which, more skilful builders constantly arose in Britain, who were instructed by the watchful (Vigilans,) remainder of the old British Architects.

Now, were first of all built, the churches in Canterbury and Rochester, and the older churches were repaired. After this, also, King Charles Martel, sent many masons over the sea to Britain, as the Saxon Kings had desired him, and thus the vigour of Architecture continually increased under the direction of the old British Architects.

It is to be regretted, it is true, that many beautiful Augustan edifices were destroyed by the incursions of the Danes, who also had burnt many records of the Society, (Societas,) with the Monastic buildings, in which, even at that time, the Lodges were already held : this want, however, the pious King Athelstane, who prized the art so much, determined to remove, when he had concluded peace with the Danes ; and to restore many splendid buildings. He commanded, therefore, that the Roman Constitution which St. Alban had introduced, should be again adopted and confirmed ; for which purpose, he also gave his youngest, *(perhaps adopted,)* son Edwin, who had joined the Architects, and learnt their customs, a charter of freedom for the Masons, that they might govern themselves, and be able to found institutions for the progress of the art. He also caused Masons to come from Gaul, and made them also Wardens, and the Constitutions of the Greeks, Romans, and Gauls, which they had brought with them in writing, were compared with those of St. Alban, and in accordance with them, all the Societies of Masons were to be arranged.

Thus, see now, in the pious Prince Edwin, your protector, who will execute the royal commands, encourage you all, and remind you not to let errors which you have before committed, occur again. For this reason the Architects and Wardens of all the Lodges must meet every year, and deliver their reports about the buildings, and what there is in the work which may be improved.

He has called you here together to 𝔚𝔬𝔯𝔨, and the Wardens shall now repeat to you the laws which they have found in the faithful old records which have been examined, and which are good and useful to observe.

But the following are the laws which you will accept and promise to observe, when you have taken them by means of laying of the hand upon the Sacred Book, *(Evangelium,)* which the Wardens will present to you.

Every Master *(Magister fabricae,)* shall cause them to be read in his Lodge. Also, every Master, shall cause them to be read, when a new Brother is admitted, because such an one, shall also swear on the Gospels to observe them.

II. 𝔗𝔥𝔢 𝔩𝔞𝔴𝔰 𝔬𝔯 𝔬𝔟𝔩𝔦𝔤𝔞𝔱𝔦𝔬𝔫𝔰 𝔩𝔞𝔦𝔡 𝔟𝔢𝔣𝔬𝔯𝔢 𝔥𝔦𝔰 𝔅𝔯𝔬𝔱𝔥𝔢𝔯 𝔐𝔞𝔰𝔬𝔫𝔰 𝔟𝔶 𝔓𝔯𝔦𝔫𝔠𝔢 𝔈𝔡𝔴𝔦𝔫.

1. The first obligation is, that you sincerely honor God, and follow the laws of the Noachedæans, because they are divine laws, which should be observed by the whole of the world : for this reason, you shall also avoid all heresies, and not sin against God thereby.

2. You shall be faithful to your King without treachery ; and without guile, obey the authorities, wherever you may find yourself. High treason, be far from you ; and if you hear of anything of the kind, you shall warn the King.

3. You shall be obliging to all men, and as far as you can, make true friendships with them ; not being hindered therefrom if they are attached to another religion or opinion.

4. In particular, you shall always be faithful to one another ; teach one another truly ; and assist one another in the art ; not speak evil one of another ; but do by each other as you would wish to be done by. Also, should a Brother offend

O

against anyone, or against his Brethren, or err in any other matter, all of you must assist him to make it right again, that he may be made better.

5. You must be faithful to the deliberations, and labours of the Members in every Lodge, and keep the sign a secret from every one who is not a Brother.

6. Every one shall refrain, from faithlessness because without faith and honesty, the Brotherhood cannot exist: and a good name is a great estate. Also, ye shall always regard the service of the Lord or Master whom ye serve, and help to promote his interests ; and always bring his work honestly to an end.

7. Ye shall always pay honestly what ye owe ; and above all, do nothing which might endanger the good repute of the Brotherhood.

8. So then no Master shall undertake any task, if he does not believe he has ability to execute it, for he would only cause the Architect shame among the Brethren. Further, every Master shall demand fair play, so that he can live, and pay his workmen.

9. Further, nobody shall seek to deprive another of the work which has been given to him, unless he is incapable of doing it.

10. Further, no Master shall take an Apprentice for any term but seven years ; and shall not, even then, make him a Mason, without the counsel and approval of the rest of his Fellow-Brethren.

11 Further, no Master or Mason, shall take the fees, to make anyone a Mason, unless he is free-born, of good repute, has capacity, and has no bodily infirmity.

12. Further, no Companion shall find fault with another, unless he knows better how to do the work, than he with whom he finds fault.

13. Further, every Master shall listen to the Architect, and every Mason to the Master, when he is required to improve his work, and to pay attention thereto.

14. Further, all Masons shall be obedient to their Officers, and do willingly what they bid them.

15. Further, every Mason shall receive Companions, who come from a distance, and who give him the Sign. He shall then care for them, as it is taught him. He shall also assist necessitous Brethren if he has received information of their distress, as he is taught, and even if it is at the distance of half a mile.

16. Further, no Master or workmen, shall admit another, who has not been made a Mason, to the Lodge, to see the art of moulding, nor let him mould stones, nor make any square or level, nor teach him the use of them.

These are the Obligations, (Laws,) which are useful and necessary to be kept. Whatever is found in future to be useful and necessary, shall be written down, and made known by the Wardens, that all the Brethren may be bound to observe it.

Here endeth the Constitution.

The Latin certificate which follows, runs thus : "This manuscript, written in the old language of the country, and which is preserved by the Venerable Architectonic Society in our town, agrees exactly with the preceding Latin translation."

I confirm this. York. Jan^{ry} 4th 1806

(*Stonehouse.*)

The undersigned, hereby certify officially, that this transcription of the Latin certificate, which forms portion of the Latin translation, that is rendered into German as above, is an exact copy of the original ; and that the German version above is a faithful reproduction is hereby declared, after comparison by three Linguists.

Altenberg. Jan 9th 1809.

Royal Chancery of Saxony

Carl Erdmann Weller

(Secretary of the Government Tribunal.)

𝕿𝖍𝖊 𝖔𝖑𝖉 𝕺𝖇𝖑𝖎𝖌𝖆𝖙𝖎𝖔𝖓𝖘 𝖆𝖓𝖉 𝕾𝖙𝖆𝖙𝖚𝖙𝖊𝖘, 𝖈𝖔𝖑𝖑𝖊𝖈𝖙𝖊𝖉 𝖇𝖞 𝖔𝖗𝖉𝖊𝖗 𝖔𝖋 𝖙𝖍𝖊 𝕶𝖎𝖓𝖌 𝖎𝖓 𝖙𝖍𝖊 𝖞𝖊𝖆𝖗 1694. 𝕿𝖍𝖎𝖘 𝖇𝖞 𝖙𝖍𝖊 𝖈𝖔𝖒𝖒𝖆𝖓𝖉 𝖔𝖋 𝖙𝖍𝖊 𝕶𝖎𝖓𝖌 (𝖂𝖎𝖑𝖑𝖎𝖆𝖒 III.)

1. The first obligation is, that you shall be faithful to God, and avoid all Heresies which contradict Him.

2. Further, you shall also be faithful subjects of your King, and obey those placed in authority by him. You shall not take part in High Treason or treachery, but give notice to the King thereof, or to his Council.

3. Further, you shall be true to all men, and particularly to each other ; instruct, and mutually assist one another : and above all, do to others, as you would they should do unto you.

4. Further, you shall diligently frequent the Lodges, in order that you may constantly receive instruction, preserve old customs, and faithfully keep everything secret which you may have learned concerning Masonry, that strangers may not enter, in an irregular way.

5. You shall also neither steal, nor hide stolen goods, but be faithful to the Lord who pays you, and to the Master for whom you work ; also see to the profit of the Lord, and work for his advantage.

6. Further, you shall love all Masons, and term them Companions or Brethren, and call them by no other name.

7. Further, you shall not seduce your Brother's wife to commit adultery, nor defile his daughter, nor his maid ; nor bring him to shame in any way : nor cause him to lose his work.

8. Further, you shall honestly pay for your food and drink, where you may turn in. You shall commit no crime, nor do anything base, by which the Society of Masons might fall into ill repute.

These are the general obligations which bind every Master Mason and his Brethren.

The particular duties are these.

Firstly. No Mason shall undertake work for a Master-builder, or anyone else, unless he knows that he is fit, and capable of completing the work ; as otherwise he will discredit the Craft.

Secondly. No Master shall at any time undertake a work for which he is not paid sufficient to permit him faithfully to serve his employer, and to enable him to live decently, and to pay his workmen properly ; but he shall not demand more than what is just. Also, no Master or Brother, shall supplant another, unless in a case where the latter has not sufficient knowledge to enable him to complete the work which he has undertaken.

Thirdly. No Master or Brother shall take an apprentice for any less period than seven years. In the same manner no Master shall make anyone a Mason, unless he has the consent of at least six or seven of his Brethren. But whoever is made a Mason must be freeborn, of good origin, and have straight and sound members, as a man should have.

Fourthly. No Master shall take an apprentice, unless he has work enough to employ two or three of his Brethren.

Fifthly. No Master of workmen shall leave his employers' work undone, or transfer it to another as day work, but faithfully and honestly complete it, whether he may have agreed by the piece or by the day.

Sixthly. Every Master shall pay his Brethren and Assistants what they have earned, that they may not disgrace him by bad work. Also, no one shall accuse another, to rob him of his good name.

Seventhly. No Brother shall speak to his fellow Brother hastily, or in an unbecoming manner, without a cause.

Eighthly. Every Mason shall behave respectfully to his Officers and Elder Brethren. Also, no Mason shall play cards, dice, hazard, or any other unlawful game, because he would thereby dishonor himself and the Craft.

Ninthly. No Brother shall rove about at night, except he be in the company of one of his Brethren, that he may be kept from improper places and deeds.

Tenthly. Every Master and Brother shall come to the Assembly, if it is within five miles of his abode, as soon as he is summoned to it; and he shall also there await the verdict of the Master and Brethren, if he has sinned against the Craft; and he shall submit himself to the punishment which the remaining Masters and Brethren impose upon him. If, however, they cannot pardon his offence, he shall be excluded from the Work.

Eleventhly. No Master or Brother shall permit anyone who cannot give the right Sign, to make a mould, or square, or draw a line, or teach him to use these things. He shall not let him enter his Lodge, nor use him to mould the stones.

Twelfthly. Every Mason shall receive lovingly, the friendly Brethren who give the right Sign, and if they want work, or ask for this only to the next Lodge as usual, he shall give to them in this manner, that if he have stones to mould he gives them half to do, and thus finds employment for them. If however he has not stones to mould, he shall assist him to the next Lodge with money.

These are the old Obligations; they shall be read according to custom, to every one who is made a Freemason.

Regulations Compiled and Arranged in order, from the written records, from the time of King Edred to King Henry VIII.

1. All lawful Brotherhoods shall be placed under Patrons who belong to the Craft, and who can give counsel to the King. Neither several Brotherhoods who join together, nor a single one, can elect a Patron for themselves.

2. They shall in the first instance be called to counsel by the King, in order that they may make proposals to the Architects in wars, and for the construction of large buildings *(Opus)* in accordance with the science and knowledge which belongs to them. Besides this, they shall work with the Architect, that great buildings may be erected to the honor of the Craft. For this reason, all men who are employed as foremen, *(Werkmeister,)* shall be previously examined.

All Patrons, Architects, Masters, and Wardens, *(Magistris et Curatoribus,)* shall assemble their Brotherhoods once every year, on a chosen day ; and undertake such examinations together ; and they shall mutually counsel each other ; and also take care that past errors are corrected ; and that the decisions in every Lodge, which may have been regarded as the peculiar laws (Crafties) of any one Lodge, may be generally accepted ; and that the lawful Brotherhoods may also always find work, and that the Lords, *(Locator operis,)* may be honestly served, and they shall always resist the entry of strangers and disturbers, who do not rightly belong to the Craft.

3. The Patron, or he who is selected by him for the purpose, shall occasionally examine the Brotherhoods in their Lodges, and take care that they continue in their work and customs ; and see that these things are done in a similar way in every Lodge.

4. It is well if the numbers of the Members of a Brotherhood are not too numerous, because, otherwise, the Wardens will be hindered in keeping good order, the numbers shall be fifty or sixty without reckoning the accepted Masons.

A note follows here: (For a long time past, the whole of them, in England and Scotland, have numbered each one hundred.)

5. If the number, of the Members of a Brotherhood, has increased so much over the proper number, that the surplus is sufficient to form a Lodge, a new Lodge shall then be formed. Members of older Lodges, whose numbers are too numerous, may join the new Lodge, if it is more convenient to them.

6. The Master of a Lodge can found a new Lodge, just so well as he can make Freemasons, and as he can open the doors of all Lodges to them.

7. The Masters who form new Lodges, shall remind the members of them, to also elect for themselves a Patron, and when this is done, they shall make their Constitutions known to all regular Lodges by charters. Every year a new Master, who presides, shall be elected. He selects his Deputies, who fill his post, if he is absent ; and Assistants are also then given him.

9. Every year, upon St. John the Baptist's Day, every Lodge shall assemble, with the Architect for whom the Members work, or with his deputies. They shall converse in a friendly manner, take counsel concerning the new Master to be elected, and take a meal together in mutual love. It shall be previously settled who shall provide for the meal, and the cost thereof shall be fixed.

10. Every presiding Master of a Lodge, shall be competent to call all the members together, as often as he may find it necessary, and all the Brethren must obey. The same may also be done by his Deputy, or by the Senior Warden, in case the Master shall be hindered from doing so. In all Lodges, every thing is decided, by a majority of the voices of those present.

11. Every Master of a Lodge, or he who is empowered to do so, shall keep a book, in which, not only the laws which are to be read at every initiation, shall be written ; but also, all remarkable matters.

12. Whoever wishes to be made a Master, must seek to become so for several months before ; and all the Brethren of the Lodge where he has so sought, shall vote. Also in an assembled Lodge, no more than five new Brethren shall be accepted at one time, in order that they may all comprehend the first instructions.

13. Whoever shows himself disobedient to his Patron or to his Superiors, or otherwise commits such a fault that his Brethren cannot be satisfied with him,

shall be admonished by the Master and Wardens, or by him who is commissioned to do so, to improve himself: When this has happened twice, no more work shall be given to him.

14. In all decisions which are arrived at in the Lodge, the old Charges, and the Marks of Secrecy shall be kept in view; for they must remain untouched, and as they are unchangeable and useful, must always be carefully observed.

———

The Latin Certificate which follows, runs thus: " This translation in the Latin language is the same as that which has been added, from time to time, to the aforesaid parchment manuscript; and which is at the end of it."

I certify this, York MDCCCVI on the same day.

(Stonehouse.)

The present copy of a Latin Certificate is the same in meaning, as the original that is among the translations of the Charges and Regulations which we translated at length above; and it is, moreover, according to the opinion of competent judges, and by the undersigned, certified to be correct, after comparison.

Altenberg, 9th January, 1809,
    Royal Chancery of Saxony,
        Carl Erdman Weller,
            Secretary of the Government Tribunal.

ABOUT THE AUTHOR

William James Hughan (1841–1911). Masonic author and scholar, Bro. Hughan is perhaps best known for his revised edition of Mackey's Encyclopedia and his many papers published in *Ars Quatuor Coronatorum.*

William Hughan was baptised in Kirkmabreck Parish on 14 August, 1806, the second son born to Samuel Hughan and Mary McKie.

Like his brother Peter, William grew up on the Hughan farm at Balhasie, near Creetown, and then moved down into England as a young man. The brothers moved to Stonehouse, in Devonshire, where they were both drapers. Samuel moved back to Scotland several years after the death of his father in 1835, and resumed farming. William, however, remained in Stonehouse, where he married and raised a family.

William Hughan married Margaret Chisholm in 1838, and their first child, Samuel Chisholm Hughan, was born the following year in 1839.

Another son, William James Hughan, followed in February of 1841, then Peter in 1844 and Mary Jessie in 1848.

Initiated: 1863
Saint Aubyn Lodge No. 954, Devonport
Master: 1868, 1878 Fortitude Lodge No. 131
Provincial Grand Secretary, 1869–1871, Cornwall
Past Senior Grand Deacon: 1874 UGLE
Past Senior Grand Warden: 1876 Egypt
Senior Grand Warden: 1874 Iowa

www.ingramcontent.com/pod-product-compliance
Lightning Source LLC
Chambersburg PA
CBHW020005290326
41935CB00007B/314